to the Colonel
Welcome to u
(

Praise for The Big Dog Diaries

"I read this book quite by accident. A friend gave it to me and while I was eating lunch one day, I casually read the first few pages and was hooked by this big ugly dog's story. Anyone who is a dog lover will fall in love with Big." - Andrew C. Palmer

"A very quick (too quick!) read. I love Laz's style. If you are looking for one of those annoyingly cloying books about a cutesy dog, try something else. If you want gritty realism, try something else. If you want a delightfully droll read, then settle in for a very pleasant time. I'm going to make this my go-to book when gifting people who like animals." - Mary L. Herrick

"I had a hard time putting [the book] down. Written in a unique style, this is a book that dog people, runners, walkers, and everybody else with a heart will enjoy." - Harald Vaessin "HEFV"

"A story about a pit bull dog may be offputting to some; but one must forget all the negative things associated with this breed in this case. Lazarus Lake is a great storyteller. His prose style is different from probably anything you have read before; but it flows smoothly and keeps the reader interested. Whether big is as special as he seems because of his genetics, or the training he received from laz, or a combination of the two is not important to the quality of the stories. He provides entertainment for his human family; and these stories shall provide great entertainment for all those fortunate enough to read them." - Dan Baglione

the big dog diaries

the big dog diaries
part 4: the big year
(summer and fall)

Lazarus Lake

bigdogdiaries.com
drystoneman@hotmail.com

First Printed Edition, September 2014

Printed in the United States of America
Print ISBN-10: 1500165492
Print ISBN-13: 978-1500165499
BISAC: Pets / Dogs / Breeds

Published by Trail Trotter Press / Run to Win, LLC (the "Publisher").

Trail Trotter Press
824 Roosevelt Trail #203
Windham, ME, 04062
www.TrailTrotterPress.com

Table of Contents

Foreward

Some might consider it divine providence that brought the Big Dog into my life. Arriving at the time he did, Big was there at just the right moments to accompany me through major transitions.

A lifelong long distance runner, I had just incurred the injury which would end that running career, and leave me with only the option to walk. At the time Big arrived, I still thought I would work my way through this problem, the same way I always had before. Big was there, with his quiet acceptance of the hand he had been dealt, along with his refusal to be less than joyous in the playing of those cards. With Big at my side, I walked into a new chapter in my life; discovering that the love of covering long distances on foot did not have to end, just because I could no longer run them.

A career accountant; at the same time as my relationship with the Big was transitioning into a partnership, I found myself involuntarily retired. While I thought I was at the peak of my career; with decades of experience to draw on, yet still vital enough that the accumulating effects of time had not begun to impact my abilities, the world had decided that I was too old to begin anew. It would have been easy to grow bitter at the perceived rejection, and wallow in self-pity at having become a member of the discarded generation. I had only to look at the Big; gentle, affectionate, and passionate in his love of people, yet treated with horror and revulsion because of the reputation of his breed, to find that option impossible. Big bore his burden with quiet dignity, I felt obligated to live up to that example. As "me and big" walked our daily patrols around the "big territory" I came to realize that we had both found ourselves a place in the world. Surrounded by the beauty of peaceful farms and woodlands, and accepted for who we are by our neighbors and friends, we really had everything we needed.

It brings a secret smile when I read the description of the Big Dog Diaries, and it refers to Big as a "rescue dog." I never rescued the Big. He showed up at my home, just when he was needed the most, and decided that he belonged to me. How he came to choose me, I will never know for sure... Big keeps his secrets well. Perhaps it really was divine providence.

My Name is Big recounts the arrival of the Big, and how he went from a tolerated presence, for whom we only wanted to find a permanent home, to a member of the family. Big Adventures and Big Tails tell the story of our journey from a mere man and his dog, to a partnership.

A partnership like ours is almost like a marriage. As "me and big" greet each day of our travel through life, there are always new adventures just around the next bend, or over the next hill. With his remarkable intelligence, and his desire to please his master, my big friend always has new surprises for me. The Big Year is just that. It is the accumulated stories of one unique year in "big territory." It begins in June, immediately following the race which concluded Big Tails. The race in which, thanks to my training under "coach big," I once again got to savor the taste of pushing myself to the limit, despite my bad leg. From there the Big Year follows us through the seasons of Summer, Fall, Winter, and Spring and back to my, now annual, June race. As usual, there is no real plot; just the daily adventures that are life with Big.

Me and big hope you enjoy our stories!

summer 2012

hello.
my name is big,
and i love the summer.

in the summer,
master gets me early every day,
so we can walk in the dark.
all the animals are out before the sun comes up.
i love to smell the animals about.
i love to walk in the dark.

in the summer,
master fills me a big pool of cool water.
when it is hot i can splash and splash.
the cool water feels so good,
that i roll in the dirt and laugh.

in the summer,
sometimes big storms come.
master brings me up on the porch,
and we sit watching the rain.
i lean against my master's leg,
and he pets me.

the summer is the perfect time of the year.

in the summer there are butterflies to chase
and biting flies to snap.
the birds sing all day,
and at night my master sits with me on the porch
and we listen to the night bugs sing.

summer is slow and lazy.
i can sleep in the sun until i am too hot.
then splash in my pool,
or sleep in the shade.

i love the summer.
i wish it lasted all year.

big

06-18-12
big aggression

little & sophie are so much simpler.
little & sophie are dogs like i always thought of dogs.

little, with her single-minded attachment to me,
sophie, with her single-minded attachment to food.
it isn't that they don't have depth.

i remember poor little, the night i forgot to tell her she could eat
& started watching tv.
it was horrible to get up and notice my poor dog,
lying in the floor where i left her an hour ago, looking mournfully
at her untouched bowl of food.
i felt so guilty that i never forgot again.

and sophie has unexpected depth.
with her here, and amy in massachusetts,
you only need to see her jump up at the slightest sound from the
back of the house
(thinking it might be amy coming home)
to appreciate what is really important to her.
she twinkle-toes off down the hall, head high, tail up, the picture
of happiness...

only to slink slowly back into the room 20 minutes later
head hanging, tail drooping, working that sad eyed look she has
mastered,
and lie back down on her bed with a loud sigh.
she is certainly, first and foremost, amy's dog.
i have no doubt that she would gladly sacrifice a food pellet to get
amy home...

maybe two.

but big.
big puts nuance into the relationship between a dog and a man.
i finally figured out what this pit bull aggression is all about,
big is passive aggressive.
the vet figured it out right away.
that first day when i went to pick up big after they treated his
gunshot wound,

4

she was telling me that "those dogs" are very centered on their owner,
when we were interrupted by loud barking that i had never heard before
(i'd recognize it anywhere now)
she looked back in the room where the animals were kept and told me;
"your boy has found his voice. he has decided you own him."
big isn't a "rescue dog"...

i am a "rescue owner."

i don't know why big chose me,
but i don't think i ever had a chance.
when big sets his mind on something, he is not going to be denied.

one of big's most prominent characteristics is his desire to please.
we work together as a team,
and i know i can absolutely rely on him in a crisis.
but during our routine walks he can be something of an imp.
he has this move i call "the squat."
when he stops to send a pee-mail, he always starts in front of me,
and speed marks so that he is done before i reach the end of the leash past him.

he has to;
balanced on 3 legs, he can't maintain equilibrium when i hit the end of the leash.
on the other hand, when he finds a particularly enticing scent,
or stops to read another dog's pee mail,
he plants all four feet and kind of squats.
when big digs in, he is not easy to move.
i hit the end of his leash and jerk to a stop.

"hey big. we aren't stopping here."
he gives me this innocent look, trots back up beside me and we continue on our way.
he is very careful not to laugh,
but i have always had a sneaking suspicion he finds this very amusing.

it fits in with his twisted sense of humor.
(remember his old game; catch me if you can)

i am more convinced that he is pulling a fast one when he does a
fake squat.
i'll catch him out of the corner of my eye, squatting over some
object in the road,
and brace myself to pull him loose instead of getting stopped in
my tracks...

and just as i lean into the leash he will start moving again.
i nearly fall on my face every time.
"did you think that was funny, big?"
big holds his deadpan expression, studying something in the
distance.

when me & big are going thru our routines alone,
he has a remarkable repertoire of things he knows how to do.
when company is around he is like goober's talking dog.
unless it involves petting, a leash, or a car-ride,
like as not big is going into his full "dumb dog" act.

earlier, when i felt guilty that i hadn't taught big any "tricks"
a number of people wrote to say that big didn't seem like that
sort of dog,
and i had to agree.

he can be goofy and silly when he is in the mood,
but he also has a sense of personal dignity.
he gladly follows commands for a purpose.
but if i try to put him thru his paces for a guest,
he is suddenly dumb as a stump.

in his mind big does not see himself as "some circus dog."
he does not like to "perform."
he is a master of "hop up"
i can tell him to "hop up" in the truck or car.
i can tell him to "hop up" on the steps,
or on a fallen tree trunk, or a rock.

the first time we went to the vet, and went over to weigh him on
the scales,
i thought we were going to shine.

i walked him over to the scales & told him to "hop up."
big just stood there looking around innocently;
"i am just a dumb dog."
i patted the scales with my hand,
a command he clearly understands to mean i want him on that
spot.
he licked my hand.

"maybe there is just too much excitement here."
i found myself making excuses.
i stepped up on the scales & big stepped up there with me.
i stepped off, and big stepped off.
i got back on, and big got on with me.
he was carefully avoiding eye contact
(a key component of his passive aggression)
but i got the feeling he was stifling a grin.

i made him sit.
i got off, and big got up and stepped off with me.
me & the vet assistant tried to push big up on the scales.
big is as wide as he is tall, and strong as an ox.
i pulled with the leash, and the girl pushed with all her might,
and we got big to go in circles all around the outside of the scales.
i put my hands on my hips and looked at big.
he wagged his tail & looked off into space;
"i'm doing my best, master, but i am only a dumb dog."

i got on the scales, and big got on with me.
i picked up one foot,
big picked up one foot.
i put my foot down,
big put his foot down.
staring off into space is not a sign that big doesn't know exactly
what is going on.
i made him "sit"
tried to get him to "stay"
and finally put my hand on top of his head and held him on the
scales long enough to get some measurement.

we went over and sat back down.
big was looking up at me and wagging his tail;
"that was fun, lets do it again!"

big is smart as a whip.
he learns new commands with a single repetition.
he is eager to please,
and has a remarkable ability to anticipate what i want.

but he also has a mind of his own.
when he doesn't want to do something,
he can play dumb with the best.
he never directly disobeys,
i just can't seem to get the right combination to accomplish what
i want.
and all the time big is wagging his tail
and carefully hiding the secret smile i know he has going on
inside...

passive aggressive.

when i think about it,
big has always been this way.
he never resisted being put in the pen.
he just unraveled the chain link fence & got out.

he didn't resist being strapped into that straight-jacket of a
harness.
and he didn't resist when i put it back on him 15 minutes later.
but he didn't look disappointed when i carted it's lifeless carcass
off afterwards.

i think tomorrow morning,
when big takes me for my walk,
i am going to have him do an extra session of "heel"...

it makes me feel like i am in charge.

laz

06-18-12
tick tape

duct tape is the ultimate runner's friend.
i use it for everything from equipment repair to blister
prevention.
but here is a use (especially if you are out on trails) which i
haven't heard mentioned.
duct tape is great for ticks.

after a warm, wet winter the ticks are terrible this year...

wait. this is middle tennessee; the ticks are terrible every year.

i keep a roll of duct tape on the table beside my chair.
i have peeled off a small strip and made it into a loop, and stuck it
on top of the roll, with the sticky side out.

whenever i find a tick on me, or feel one crawling across me,
i pull it off and stick it on the duct tape.
there is no escape, not even for a tick.
when it fills up, i throw it away and make a new loop.

this is really handy, because ticks are sneaky varmints.
they show up not only immediately after a run,
but hours later, even after i have showered and changed.
having dogs makes it even worse.
but dog ticks can go on the same duct tape.

later in the year, when the seed ticks start showing up
i sometimes run into a bunch of them and have the little suckers
crawling all over me.

it is hard as heck to pick them off by hand,
but a strip of duct tape can be applied and removed
and it will pick up every seed tick it touches.
i can clear myself of seed ticks in only a few minutes.

one caveat.
sandra does seem to have some issues with my roll of duct tape...
and the speckling of ticks waving their legs about in futility.
women are sometimes repelled by the strangest things.

but even she recognizes how much better it is that the ticks are fastened there...

as opposed to hiding in the house, waiting for a chance to attach to her.

laz

06-20-12
big wheaties

where i grew up, they called it "feeling your wheaties."
a horse might break into a furious sprint,
a cow might be bouncing around, shaking its head and kicking up its heels,
a boy might go charging down a ravine, bouncing off the walls.

we all know what it feels like,
that sudden burst of energy and high spirits.

now big has always had an excess of "wheaties."
exuberance is part of his everyday world,
and i had been feeling sorry for him.
it has been so hot that the most fun he gets is splashing in his pool.
(which has gunga din here hauling gallons and gallons out to keep it filled)

yesterday his high spirits just ran over,
and he couldn't keep them contained any more.

i have a time block reserved for big in the early evening,
once the sun gets low and it starts to cool down some.
he comes up on the porch and eats,
but we also have time for some petting,
we might walk around the yard & look at my latest rock project,
and always, always he likes to spend some time lying on his
tattered sleeping bag on the porch while we talk,
or just sit and listen to the woods.
this is on big's schedule, and he looks forward to it all day.

so he is always excited to see me coming to get him.
we have a routine for the walk back to the house.
first he has to "HEEL"
after he has politely heeled part way, i tell him "OK"
and he is off like a shot,
skidding into his 90 degree turn at the steps
(big can turn on a dime, but even big can't do it on loose gravel)
taking one bound up to the landing,
and a second bound up onto the porch,

11

running over to where his food is sitting on a table
and standing on his hind legs to see what he has,
before coming back to wait for me at the top of the steps.

while big is "wooo wooo wooing" and waiting for me to get there
to let him loose
his moods range from ecstatic to nearly delirious with joy.
yesterday he was busting-out-of-his-skin ecstatic,
and i decided to give him a break in the routine.
he was waiting for me to go, so he could fall into place for the
"HEEL"
and instead i told him;
"why don't you just go on ahead today, mr big?"
he looked up at me, incredulous.
"it's alright big, just go on to the porch."
i didn't have to tell him again,
the big was off like a shot.

after he checked on his food, tho,
big was really feeling his wheaties,
and he spontaneously erupted into a round of bigsprints.

bigsprints are an amazing sight,
a remarkable combination of power and agility.
to see this block of muscle executing 180's at top speed,
suddenly stopping stock still,
and then accelerating back into top speed.
the big guy is simply an astounding athlete.

yesterday he was especially lit up,
he kept going faster and faster.
the sight of this dog,
mouth wide open, lips curled back, tongue flapping out the side
of his mouth,
eyes so wide that i could see the whites all the way around,
he was wearing his insane-dog-clown face.

i couldn't help laughing,
which only seemed to spur him on further.

he added a new manouever,
turning a full-speed 90 at the top of the steps and taking one
giant bound to the ground past the end of the steps,

then a second huge bound all the way to the edge of the woods,
where he would land stock still, like a statue.
no human gymnast has ever executed a landing so perfect,
decelerating from full speed to motionless without the slightest
dip to absorb the impact.

after about 1 second motionless,
he would spin and take one giant leap back to the bottom of the
steps,
and a second to the landing,
where he would spring off all four feet and literally soar over the
top of the steps,
landing almost at the back door, and turning into the next
bigsprint without slowing down.
what a show.
i laughed all the way to the bottom of the steps.

i stopped at the bottom of the steps to watch.
i figured i'd let him go until he could go no more.
it did my heart good to see the big guy having so much fun.
i didn't know just how much fun he had in mind.

after a couple more laps of the porch,
big suddenly turned that 90 at the top of the steps again.
in a flash i found myself looking at a 90 pound block of muscle
hurtling thru the air directly at me,
that insane-dog-clown grin, and wide eyes higher than my head.

now, we all have those moments,
when circumstances call on us to think at an accelerated pace.
the instant emergency when it seems like we can think a
thousand things in a hundredth of a second.
when our whole lives can flash in front of our eyes.
if you have been rescued by a big, you have some extra moments
like that, and this was one of those moments.

i had instinctively started to jump back when big went airborne.
if he hit me at that speed, he would knock me into next week.
simultaneously i thought thru all the possibilities.
big could be playing "chicken," counting on me to get out of the
way.
or he could be playing "can i make master wet his pants?"

and already know how he was going to avoid the seemingly inevitable collision.

chicken is not big's style,
so i froze, stopping myself from jumping back.
my best chance was to trust big's incredible body control and his ability to change directions
(altho how he would do that in midair... i had no idea)

my mind was racing so fast, i had time to hope i made the right choice,
before i heard big's front feet hit the bottom step.
it was just enough to change his course & save me from a couple of broken legs.

big apparently doesn't feel the need to build a lot of cushion into his tricks.
i might have just felt the wind of his passage,
or he might have actually brushed my clothes as he went past behind me.
but either way i remained unscathed.
(had i tried to jump back he would have pasted me)

shaken, but unscathed,
as big landed behind me,
he then made a last leap to the edge of the woods.

he didn't hold his landing (for the judges) this time,
but instead turned to look at me.

i don't care what anyone says, that dog can laugh.
and he was laughing harder than i have ever seen him laugh.
it was a side-splitting, table pounding laugh.
i half expected to see tears come out of the corners of his eyes.

big can't actually talk,
but sometimes you can hear what he is thinking.
at that moment his expression clearly said;
"you should have seen the look on your face!!!"
how could i not laugh with him?

after we both regained our composure he came over and looked up at me for instructions.

big has learned good stairway manners.
i will either tell him to go on ahead & wait at the top,
or have him wait at the bottom until i am up,
and then follow.
stairway manners are good when you don't want to trip over
your dog.

this time i told him;
"aw, come on big guy. lets walk up together."
and we did.

laz

06-24-12
the last big story

every time i relate one of big's stories i wonder if that might be
the last.
after all, most of the original conflicts have been resolved.
the big personality seems to have won over his most entrenched
opponents.
(i can't time our workouts any more,
because we don't ever have a walk that someone doesn't stop to
pet the big guy.)
pit bulls are supposed to be the feared terrors of their
neighborhood.
big has made friends for miles around and must be the most
popular dog in the whole short creek area.
even sandra (who might never admit it) has come to love the big,
happy fella.

i might not be able to foretell another adventure in the making
(i suppose they wouldn't be adventures if i knew what was
coming)
but life with a big is a fresh adventure every day.

if we never actually won the battle of containment,
big has at least discontinued his wide ranging solo adventures.
he only lets himself loose when he feels like we are getting
behind schedule,
and then all he does is come to the porch to remind me it is time
to go.

big has important work to do,
and he doesn't like to procrastinate.
he isn't about to let me drag him down.

this morning was one of those times that i just wasn't moving
quickly enough.
i was sitting on the porch putting on my running shoes,
big was out in his area, loudly telling me that i was far too slow...

then he got quiet.
and a quiet big is an ominous portent.
when big gets quiet i can only hope that he is patiently waiting.

a moment later there was a loud "THUMP" as he hit the bigloo
with his front paws.
the big piledriver move is something i have never seen another
dog do, but it is highly effective for a dog with the big block of
muscle build,
and the "THUMP" was followed by the sound of his bigloo
skidding across the ground.
the next sound i heard was unfamiliar; a loud "POP."
but when big came thundering around the corner, trailing a short
segment of his cable,
i knew what it had been.

it was the sound of yet another "240 pound dog" cable meeting
its end at the paws of a 90 pound big.
i was left to wonder if the bigloo skidding was part of his cable
snapping technique,
since we still haven't caught him in the act.
it is generally impossible to figure out how big manages his
amazing feats,
unless we actually see him perform them.
and you have to be pretty sneaky to get the drop on a big.

be that as it may,
that big face was beaming as he executed his 90 degree turn at
the steps
bounded up to the porch in two prodigious leaps
and trotted over to me.
he turned around, wedged his wide backside between my feet,
and sat down facing the woods.
then he leaned back until he was pretty much laying in my lap,
his huge, red nose pointing at the sky.
his twinkling eyes looking into mine clearly said;
"i need my throat rubbed."

so we took care of some throat rubbing,
then he sat back up straight, tilted his head to one side,
and put one cheek into "cheek scratching" position.
life with big is life with laughter.

big led me thru a wide range of favorite rubs and scratches,
me laughing as i complied,
before i finally told him;

"if we're gonna get our walk in before it is baking hot, we need to get started."
and i picked up his leash.

second behind his ability to hear your eyes open in the morning,
is his ability to hear so much as a single finger touching his leash.
big started spinning in circles like a crazed gyroscope.

that was a new maneuver to me,
but i had to tell him;
"big, i can't attach your leash while you are spinning. you have to SIT!"
it took him a couple of tries.
he'd stop spinning and put his butt to the ground
(big can't really "sit" while his leash is attached, but with an effort he can hold his butt on the ground)
but when i reached out with the leash the excitement would overwhelm him
and he'd pop up and start spinning again.

once i got him fastened, we still had to negotiate the steps.
he knew to stop at the top,
altho i reminded him to "WAIT" while i went down to the landing.
when i stopped at the landing and gave him his "OK"
big rocketed down the steps.
having been thru this before i was ready.
the moment his front feet touched the landing i commanded;
"STOP!"
big stopped so fast that his back end went up in the air.

now, we have done this a thousand times,
and he *always* has to stop on the landing.
he still hits the landing at 60 miles an hour.
if i am not poised to tell him "STOP" the moment his front feet touch...

i will regret it.

we repeat the process for the lower flight of steps.
again the timely "STOP" is critical.
big anticipates many things,

but he always thinks we might start today's walk at 60 miles an hour.

big stops, almost toppling onto his nose again,
and looks back over his shoulder at me,
waiting for the word...

"now big fella, lets start our walk."
and there we go, just like every other morning.
big is turned sideways.
as if his back end has a mind of its own,
while he has his front end slowed down to our official walking speed,
the back end still wants to go 60 miles an hour.
it takes all the way around the house for him to finally get it under control.
and off we go down the tree tunnel that is our driveway,
to see what fresh adventures await us today.

the funny thing is, i started out to write about the adventures of today's walk.
lots of big things happened, but now i have used up all my time,
and i need to go to town to buy yet another replacement cable.
i have it down to a routine.
the first replacement i use their return policy.
the cables are really supposed to last for more than a month...
on a dog only 1/3 of the rated weight.
i pay for every other cable,
figuring that 2 cables per purchase is enough.
big is still a costly dog.

maybe when i get back i will have time to tell what happened out on the road today.
i hate when i get behind, because then i have some new
adventure to write about, and the old one gets forgotten.

that is life with the big.
he is never boring;
he never runs out of new tricks,
and he never runs out of new adventures.

laz

06-25-12
the rest of the "last" big story

once me & big finally got to the road it was to prove a most
interesting day.
a summer day.
a full heat summer day.
but every day is interesting in short creek.

we had no sooner reached the end of the driveway than we
found rabbit fur scattered about in the road.
big looked around to see if the stomach fairy had left anything for
him, but there was not a trace of the rabbit, besides his hair.

me & big had decided that the reason the short hares had such a
bad attitude was the food chain.
rabbits have a special place on the food chain...
they are food. everything eats them.
coyotes eat them, bobcats eat them, the hawks eat them, snakes
eat them.
with such a perilous (and generally short) life,
the short hares seem to delight in taunting big and tempting fate.
why not?
What do they have to lose?

this morning the evidence of the rabbits' primary function was
scattered all over the road.

as we started down the hill alongside the brothers farm, we
spotted a couple of donkeys up ahead.
i was glad to see them
we hadn't seen them in a long while, and wondered if mr
brothers might have gotten rid of them.

he doesn't actually raise burros,
a couple had simply showed up in his pasture a few years back.
he assumed they had wandered in from the back of his property,
where thousands of acres of woodlands lie between his place and
lynch hill road on the other side of the hills.
since then, his herd had slowly grown to number 8 burros.
i had finally heard one calling a few nights back, so i knew they
weren't all gone.

once we reached them, we found there were actually 3 donkeys,
a couple of the younger jennys and one of the mature females.
to our delight, she had a brand new foal with her.
it stood there watching us pass,
as cute as only a baby donkey can be,
gangly, knobby kneed legs and outsized ears;
and those big, dark eyes framed by long lashes.
it was a beautiful animal.
i reckon this fall, when we will find them all together again, there
will be 9.
donkeys live a long time, but don't reproduce very fast.

big & i continued on into the heat.
as we neared the former wheat fields,
we came on another scattering of rabbit fur in the road.
boy, it had been a tough night for the short hares.
big really snuffled about this time,
but again, there was nothing left but patches of hair.

when we reached the wheat fields, i winced.
after the wheat was harvested, ben had put in soybeans
and now they were sprouting.
we had a wet winter & early spring,
and as a result the wheat and the first cutting of hay had been
fabulous and early.
however, may had been abnormally dry,
and all we had so far in june was a sparse sprinkling the day after
the durby...
not even enough to settle the dust.
combined with the early heat, a year that had started with such
promise was threatening to turn grim.

fortunately, no one in big territory had put out corn this year.
the young corn has been severely affected by the dry heat,
and it appears likely the corn harvest will fall somewhere
between disastrous and nonexistent.
a second cutting of hay is unlikely, as the fields are turning
brown and dying.
and now we are counting down the days until the soybeans are
ruined as well.
we need rain in the worst way.

the soybeans we pass fall into three planting times.
those which were the first crop in that field got started before it
stopped raining.
the plants were big enough to both shelter the ground some, and
withstand a little more dry weather.
those which followed the first hay cutting got started when there
was still moisture in the ground.
they look pretty poor, but there are plants.

however, the planting that followed the wheat harvest has gotten
nothing.
the tiny sprouts we saw among the wheat stubble need rain, and
soon.
they are not strong enough to live for long in this weather.
i had sort of hoped it was dry enough they would wait for rain
before coming up.
no such luck.

every morning we look at the weather forecast before heading
out, and every morning it shows an unbroken string of hot, dry
days ahead.
then we go out and hurt for the farmers whose crops we are
watching wither in the sun.
when big kicks up his rooster tails of dirt, huge clouds of dust
float away.
and i am having a slow time recovering from the durby.
unless it rains, big won't give me a day off.

so big and i were pretty morose as we walked thru the baking
fields towards the woods.
with it not even getting cool at night
big was huffing and puffing from the heat already.
my legs were flat and tired, and i had developed a persistent ache
in my bad knee.

just before we re-entered the shade
what did we find but a third scattering of rabbit fur.
big was snuffling about furiously.
"what happened out here last night?"
big just looked at me, and gave no answer.
he and his nose knew what had killed so many rabbits.
i could only speculate.

but i did notice that, unlike every other morning,
we had yet to see a single live rabbit.
of course we hadn't seen any dead ones either,
just scattered fur.
the short hares were in hiding.

later in the walk, passing another field of wheat stubble and
withering soybean sprouts,
we came on the largest turkey creche i have ever seen.
by this time of the year, the little turkeys are about the size of
chickens.
the mothers, and single adult females form back into flocks,
and the little turkeys form large creches that accompany them.
i could see a dozen or so adult turkeys walking thru the wheat.
the young birds, still brown, were invisible.
none the less,
with this many adults i was figuring there would probably be
close to 100 babies following along.
the flock was angling across the field,
and appeared to be on track to intercept us on up the road.
big had no clue, as they were still a good distance away,
and the weeds alongside the road blocked his vision.

as we continued to converge with the flock,
i kept expecting the turkeys to spot us and peel off.
big was still clueless.
head down in his grim heat walk.
the birds were pre-occupied, stopping to scarf up loose grain that
had escaped the combine,
as well as plentiful insects,
then continuing to move.
i reckoned that the only thing visible above the weeds was my
head,
and my straw hat must have been fairly effective camouflage.

they got so close that i could see the adults well,
and even got an occasional glimpse of a young turkey crossing
bare ground.
i wondered what would happen when they reached the road and
saw us.

the first turkey came out of about 15 feet in front of us.
he was stunned to find a man and a big red bear almost on top of
him, and took off running before taking flight.

now, turkeys don't fly for fun.
i know it, and the turkeys know it.
the sound of that first bird taking flight had the same effect on
the flock as a spark has on gasoline vapors.
something on the order of a hundred wild turkeys took flight at
once with a tremendous roar of flapping wings.
big was galvanized, with the big birds flying over and around us
in all directions...
low.
he jumped back and forth frantically,
as his prey response was overwhelmed by the sheer number of
unexpected targets.
i had to laugh at the big guy
while recognizing just how effective the flocking strategy of
defense really is.

10 seconds later there was not a turkey in sight,
and we were trying to compose ourselves for the rest of the walk.

the rest of the walk was relatively uneventful.

we saw another, more normal sized, flock of turkeys.
but they spotted us from a distance and moved off into the
woods...
we never saw any of the babies that were certainly along.

the goat corner dog barely even acknowledged us by raising her
head up and looking.
then she flopped back down.
it was a day fit only for lying in the dirt.

we came on an ancient siamese cat that we'd never encountered
before.
it must have been deaf,
because it never saw us until we passed on the other side of the
road.
big's request for permission to go eliminate it was halfhearted.
and while he did leave it a pee mail, he didn't bother with a
rooster tail.

we passed by big's favorite herd of milk cows,
but they had taken refuge under the trees on the other side of the
pasture.
the cow with a crush on big was the only one to come out and
look at us, and even she only came part way.

big ignored her as usual.
and this day he didn't even leave her a pee mail.
big was fixed on finishing the walk and splashing in the cool
water in his pool.

i laughed as i remembered the one day last week that his admirer
wasn't there.
they must have milked late, and all the cows were still up around
the milk barn.
big always studiously ignores his girlfriend,
as she walks alongside the other side of the fence watching him.
then leaves her a pee mail before we turn away.

the day she was missing, he looked for her the whole way
alongside the field,
and even stopped twice to leave pee mails.
he isn't half as cool as he tries to act.

once we finally made it to the house, we only spent a few
minutes on the porch before big went to the steps to let me know
he was ready to go.
it was too hot to eat,
and while he did make time to get a little petting,
he was more than ready to splash himself in his pool
and go lay in the shade.

it is going to be a long summer if we don't get some rain.

laz

06-27-12
the big temple half marathon

one by one, me & big have been knocking off the roads around here.
the latest to fall was hoover gap road.

now that dale & linda have joined team big,
the long "runs" have become team big events.

today had been set aside for one of those new routes;
from short creek to hoover gap and back.
while it isn't actually a half marathon in length,
it is shorter than a marathon.
we figured the round trip would take about 5 hours.
the only issue was what part big could take.
big thinks anything above freezing is a hot weather event,
and we had been seeing temps up around 100.
me & big had been doing our 2 hour walks early,
(cooking big's butt in the process)
and then i had been doing 4 or 5 hours of rockwork in the afternoon
(cooking my butt in the process)

sandra had been telling me i shouldn't take big out in this heat.
he does collapse on the back porch, panting furiously, when we get home,
but she doesn't understand how the ultrarunning mind works.
big would rather die than miss a workout.

i wanted to start at about 0300 and get in before the heat was intolerable.
dale & linda have not yet conquered the need to sleep.
they were willing to go at 0530.

so sandra and i had a heated discussion on the porch last night.
i was trying to convince her to come pick big up a couple of hours into the run.

she was protesting that i should not take him at all.
big was looking from one of us to the other,
that solemn look on his face.

naturally he could not understand the discussion,
after all; he is only a dog.
only couples with a lot of years under their belt might
understand,
but the discussion finished with no spoken resolution.

i knew i was going to take big.
sandra knew i would take big.
i knew she would come and get him halfway.
she knew that if he wasn't out in his bigloo when she got up, she
would come get him.
now, if it were me who would suffer with no ride,
i would just have to suffer,
and she would ride me about it when i finally got home.
non-running ultra spouses have been known to lose their
sympathy for running foolishness.
but she loves big.

none the less, i made plans to carry the four half liter bottles in
my liquipak.
i was pretty sure i could get big home on that if i misread sandra.
with all those 5 hour days in 100 plus temps behind me,
(only taking a drink every 2 hours)
i was confident i could finish the walk without any fluids if i
needed to.

big may be smart,
but he doesn't get the unspoken agreement thing yet.
when i came out at 0500 to head out to meet dale & linda,
big didn't wait to see if he was included.
he took off his cable and came running around to meet me on the
porch...

i'm sure it has to be a coincidence that he chose this morning to
take off his cable.
he couldn't have understood our conversation.
he is only a dog, right?

we got to the place we were joining up with dale & linda first,
so me & big sat in the road and took a break while we waited.
in just a few minutes we heard lynnor's pug barking,
heralding the imminent arrival of the remainder of the big team.

the sun was just peeking over the distant hills
as we came around the corner in front of the brothers place,
where the panoramic view of our entire course was spread out in
front of us.
if linda had a camera, she'd have taken 50 pictures.
i didn't tell her this is why me & big like to be on the road every
day when the sun comes up.

instead i was thinking back a couple of years,
to when me & big watched a sunrise just like this one,
from this exact spot,
on the last day before he left "forever" to his home in st louis.
i was grateful for the fate that had reunited us.

the course was everything we had hoped for.
beautiful hills, few houses, and rarely a passing vehicle.
no matter how many times you have driven a road,
there is so much more to be seen when you pass on foot.
team big passed the time with pleasant conversation
and drinking in the sights.
big took point and attended to the all important tasks of
committing his new territory to memory...
and marking it so that lesser dogs would understand;
"this is big's road!"

a little past halfway out there was a brief crisis.
two women came out of one of the few houses to start their
morning walk.
this put them behind us,
and as far as big was concerned we were being pursued.

big's first idea was that we should flee and hide in the woods...
instead we took the easy way out,
stopping in a shady spot and letting them pass.
we must have been quite a sight as they went by;
the devil dog sitting, while linda petted him and assured him that
everything was all right.
they didn't look frightened,
but neither did they show any interest in coming over to pet the
cute puppy.

naturally, once they were in front of us big thought we should
speed up.

big is supposed to be in front.
fortunately they didn't go much further before turning and
starting back.

nearing the turnaround we passed the mystery building.
it is a huge place, like some sort of giant church out in the woods.
but the architecture is unfamiliar and there are no signs
indicating its nature.
a small garden, and a large pavilion with lots of picnic tables give
no clue as to its purpose.
local rumors are that it is a mosque, and people are suspicious as
to its intentions.

then we crossed the interstate on an overpass.
when we got above the first traffic lane,
i braced myself for big to try to run away.
i nearly toppled when he instead ran over and stuck his head
thru the rail for a better look.
big found the traffic fascinating.
you don't always know what a big is going to think.

at the turnaround it was starting to get pretty warm.
dale found a fast-food cup in the ditch and fashioned a drinking
bowl for big.
big drank a half liter with dispatch.
i had expected to see sandra by this point,
so i was grateful that i had carried extra water.
it was still going to be a long walk back.

when we reached the "mosque" we saw that there were a couple
of cars there.
dale & linda haven't been hardened by journey running,
and weren't excited at the prospect of simply going down and
knocking on doors.
but i wanted to find out exactly what that place really was.

so me & big took a detour while the rest of team big waited on
hoover gap road.

after not getting any answer at the front door,
we walked around back.
there we found a glassed in lobby area,
with three older people inside.

my questions were pretty well answered before we even reached the door.
the three people watching us were obviously indian,
and all had the telltale red spot on their forehead.
dollars to donuts, our "mosque" would turn out to be a hindu temple.

the occupants were the ones with questions,
as a sweaty, bearded homeless man with a huge pit bull was approaching their door.
fortunately for me, listers rajeev and naresh have helped me out with appropriate cultural greetings.
as i came up the last step i gave the worried residents my biggest smile,
made my best approximation of putting my hands together
(considering the impediment of big's leash)
bowed my head slightly, and said;
"namaste!"

the faces of the people inside were transformed.
both men smiled even bigger than i had, and responded with a proper "namaste."
of course, they weren't hindered by a big attached to one arm.

i have to admit, the woman did not warm up so much.
she kept her eyes on big and never did smile.
it was indeed a hindu temple,
and i was invited in to see it,
which i had to decline on account of the dog.
they suggested tying the big fella outside.
i told them he would be frightened if i left him tied up in a strange place.
(better than telling them that tying big up would be an exercise in futility)
of course indians are among the most hospitable people on earth,
and i couldn't leave until i had been given a handful of nuts,
and what seemed to be the lead man had gotten a small bowl
containing a yellow substance in what appeared to be some sort of oil,
and dabbed a small amount on my forehead.
later i found that the "spot" was red instead of yellow...

and naturally not so much a "spot" as a smear on my sweating forehead.
i am sure that they were distressed that they had not been prepared for this apparition that appeared to come out of the woods.

i left with lots of questions to ask naresh.
wondering if outsiders are permitted to attend services
(or do they have services?),
and if naresh would come along to assure that i not commit some ghastly offense!

not long after leaving the temple sandra showed up.
big was plenty happy to hop in the front seat.
he loves car rides, and there was air conditioning...
blowing right in his laughing face.

after that, the remainder of team big moved along.
i ended up drinking a total of about 12 ounces of fluid.
but, as i have said, the body can learn to store extra fluid.
i did catch myself always looking ahead as if big were still along.
operating as a team has become such a natural part of my "running" that i cannot look down the road without thinking of us both.

we beat our five hour time,
and the big started barking at us to hurry when we were still a half mile from home.
once we arrived, the whole team big convened on the back porch to rehash the adventures of the big temple half marathon.
these are good times in short creek.
we have a big to remind us that every day is the best day of our life.

laz

06-28-12
feeding hummingbirds

i got chewed out by a hummingbird yesterday.

i had gone out to sit on the front porch for a while and look out into the woods.
it was kind of a drowsy hot day
and after the big temple half marathon i was feeling sort of worn,
so i ended up leaning back in my chair with my eyes shut.

my reverie was interrupted by a chittering sound.

i opened my eyes to find a hummingbird hovering about 5 feet in front of my face...
scolding me to beat sixty.
i saw that sandra's hummingbird feeder was empty,
and i guessed that i was getting blamed.
i figured that i ought to refill it.
i enjoy watching the little guys buzz around and squabble over the feeder.
and sometimes they come around back
and buzz by me & big while we are sitting on the porch.
big will be about half asleep, and one of the hummers will whiz past his head...
the sound-sensitive big will about jump out of his skin.
i owe them something for the amusement.
and how hard can it be to fill a hummingbird feeder?

so i went and looked in the fridge.
sure enough, i found an old mayonnaise jar half full of red liquid.
i was certain that was the right stuff.

i took down the feeder and screwed off the top.
there was no opening, apparently the feeder was essentially an upside-down jar.
so i turned it over, and started unscrewing the bottom.

red liquid poured out all over my hands and started forming a puddle on the porch.
i turned it back over real quick,
but even more liquid poured out; now that the bottom was loose.

for an empty feeder, it sure had a lot of juice left.
cursing, i flipped it back, took off the bottom as fast as i could and
set it on our little tray-table.
there was enough in my jar to fill the feeder about halfway.
when i retrieved the bottom,
i found it sitting on the tray-table in a spreading red puddle,
but i picked it up and replaced it on the feeder anyway,
spilling even more juice on my hands and the porch in the
process.

then i flipped the whole device back upright,
thinking that would be the end of my problems....

each of the three little flowers now sported a stream of red juice
shooting into the air.
it sprayed my shirt, and spread streams of red fluid across the
porch as i hurried to hang it up.
for a few minutes i had a lovely red fountain.
i watched it as the fluid level gradually receded,
and as it got lower, the force of the streams gradually
diminished.
soon i had a sticky, but empty feeder.
i figured the ants were going to be overjoyed...
at least the ones that hadn't been drowned in sugar water.

it was time to step back and admire my handiwork.
there was a big, red puddle on the tray table;
several large puddles on the porch;
my hands and arms were red and sticky almost to the elbow;
streamers of red adorned my white shirt;
and there hung the feeder...
still empty, but good and sticky.

now it was time to try and at least return things to the state in
which they were when i began.
that is stage two on many of my projects.
i went around back, filled big's milk jugs with water, and got the
broom.
the feeder was relatively easy to clean.
the porch was more of an issue.
neither sandstone, nor mortar, willingly surrendered the red
stain.

as i poured more and more water on,
and swept it vigorously with the broom.
the red stain did get lighter....
as it spread over an ever growing portion of the porch.

my luck was little better with the tray-table,
altho i did avoid spreading the stain.
i discovered the stain wouldn't even come off my skin.

i have to say that this was a job well-done.
a third of the front porch was now dyed red.
the broom was dyed red.
the tray-table was dyed red.
my hands and forearms were dyed red.
and i had a pattern of random red stripes on my white shirt.
with any luck, later on i might be able to dye a whole load of
laundry red.
and the feeder was still empty...

mission accomplished.
the most important phrase a man has to learn in life is;
"i meant to do that."

when sandra got home,
i told her that her hummingbird feeder was empty.
her response?
"i don't have time to fill it right now, there is some stuff in the
fridge you can fill it with."

i am just staying off the front porch.
the hummingbirds think i am a moron.

laz

06-30-12
the big heat wave

arizona came to tennessee this week.

we have our heat, but it is always accompanied by humidity.
having spent my early years out west, i am quite familiar with
dry heat.
i was well aware that the effect is not the same, degree by degree.
90 and dry is not so bad. 90 and humid is murderous.
what i never knew before was that it is the humidity that holds
the temperatures down.
this week we have heat without the humidity and it is killing
heat.

yesterday hit 105, and i feel guilty that big lived thru it outdoors.
i have kept a close eye on him all thru the heat wave,
and at 100 i saw him splashing in his pool and then rolling
around in the dirt having a good time.
at 105 he was pretty miserable,
and knowing today would be hotter still, i cleared a place for him
in the garage and planned to bring him out of the blast furnace
by the time it reached 100.

we've been leaving on our walks early enough to get home
around sunrise,
but this morning it was still in the 80's up on the hill.
fortunately there was some cooler air down in the low places,
so the whole walk wasn't miserable.

we did meet a bicyclist riding in the dark.
(everyone knew this would be a day of killing heat)
for the rest of the walk, big kept looking over his shoulder.
his greatest fear is having bicycles sneak up on him from behind.
i often wonder what happened in his past, to create such a fear.
but that, like so many of his physical scars, is shrouded in
mystery.

he does know that bicycles come with people.
he doesn't fear anything except people.
in his big mind, aggression against people is the ultimate taboo.
for other things that hurt him, the effect is the opposite of fear.

i have been worried about walking in the dark since the skunk
incident.
skunks are the only wildlife that i can't count on fleeing if we
walk up on them in the dark.
skunks aren't inclined to flee.
but big always let me know something was there,
and we could avoid them.

now when big sees a skunk, he wants to go after it.
i tried to reason with him;
"big, you don't want to chomp on skunks."
he looked up at me with eyes that said;
"don't you remember what that stink cat did to me?"
"but big; look what you did to him. you killed him!"
big just went back about his business.
obviously i don't understand.

i saw him snap a bee out of the air one day,
and the surprised look on his face when it stung him.
now he goes after every bee he sees.
and his technique for snapping and tossing a bee with a shake of
his head prevents most of them from stinging him.

this makes me worry twice as much about skunks.
big seldom makes the same mistake twice,
and if he doesn't get sprayed by the next skunk...
who is most likely to "take one for the big team?"

ever since the buzzard "scared" amy
(who still swears she was not frightened)
big has held a relentless hate for buzzards.

despite his usually discriminating eye for other animals
(he doesn't use bee technique on flies, even horseflies, altho he is
death on biting flies)
he recognizes horses and cows, goats and sheep, and burros as
distinct animals.
he hates rabbits, and is indifferent to squirrels
(unless they get too close to one of his hidden bones.)
but he remains convinced that turkeys are sprinting ground
buzzards.

it is easy enough to guess the source of his animosity towards cats.
i can just see a trusting puppy
(and big was surely once a puppy)
taking a full raking swat across the nose.
big would never forget.

but people are different. they are his gods.
loving people is the very essence of his being.

the first rays of sunlight didn't strike us until we were nearly home, but they sliced into us like lasers.
this was going to be a day of killing heat.

it passed 100 before noon, and i set about getting big to safety.
i pulled my truck out of the garage,
and brought in his blue blanket and water bowl off the porch.
then i went to get big.
he was laying wrapped around his pool, using the mud from his splashing to help keep him cool.
that didn't stop him from coming out to greet me.

he looked surprised when i unhooked his cable.
i reckon he didn't have anything on his schedule.
"i'm going to take you to the garage to get out of this heat, big guy."
big set off at a trot, the best he can muster in the stifling heat.
i figured he was just heading for the porch,
but was surprised when he passed the steps.
surely that dog didn't know what i was talking about.
he has never been in the garage!

i was almost relieved to see him head for the truck.
ah, he'd heard me pull it out earlier,
and figured we must be going for a ride.
when i passed the truck, he went to the head of the driveway and turned to watch me.
maybe we were going for another walk.
so what if the 100 degree heat would kill him?
big is good for whatever i want him to do.
i passed the driveway, so he trotted back ahead to wait for me by my partially completed rock walls.
sometimes he gets to come watch me work.

the door to the garage was his last guess,
but he got there right behind me.
now, i am used to little, who has been taught to wait permission
to go thru doors.
(i have that thing about not wanting to trip over my dog)
so i automatically turned and gave big the "OK" to come in...
big was already halfway in.
he paused uncertainly at the "OK" and then went on in.

big never ceases to amaze me.
i have gotten used to him being a one rep learner,
but he exceeded that today.
inferring from the permission command that he was supposed to
wait before going thru the door,
he waited politely every other time we went in or out.
that gave me pause.

inference is a darn complex thought process.
i have been amazed at his ability to learn by category.
i told him once not to pee on a rock wall.
he never pees on ANY of my rock walls.
i told him once not to pee on my car tire.
he never pees on any car tires parked in our driveway...
altho he still thinks cars anywhere else are fair game.

but inference...
from a dog?
maybe i need to take another look for that zipper.

i don't know exactly how hot it got today,
i know it topped 108 by mid-afternoon.
the maple leaves literally turned yellow and curled up.
i saw a baby bird fall out of a nest.
i went to look at it, and it gasped a few times and died.
when i picked it up it felt like it had come out of the oven.
my heart bleeds for the animals in the fields and forests of short
creek.
they are made for tennessee heat.
they are built to tolerate suffocating humidity.
arizona is killing them.

laz

07-04-12
naresh joins team big

"they" say that dogs are good judges of character,
that dogs "always know."

maybe big gave up that dog ability
in exchange for his uncanny, nearly human intelligence.
because naresh is as kind a soul as big will ever meet,
and big has met him many times.
the meetings have always ended up the same;
naresh petting big and big loving it.
but the result has only been internal conflict for big.

he recognizes naresh.
he wants to run to naresh to be petted,
but he is still afraid, and also wants to run away from naresh.
because one of his greatest, and most ingrained fears
is the fear of dark skinned men.

however, the one thing he hasn't done before
is take naresh on a walk as part of the big team.
the walk isn't just an important part of big's world,
it is the most important part.
the walk is his job.
to walk with big is to become a part of his inner circle.
to walk with big is to see him truly in his element.

we hadn't gone 50 yards from the driveway before we saw
headlights coming towards us.
we crossed the road to get out of the lane with "traffic," as we
always do.

but big hung near the center line, wagging his tail.
he knows his cars by the sound of their motors.
as the car got close, it slowed,
and a familiar voice called out;
"hello big!"

it was the newspaper lady.
"come give me a kiss, mr big."

and big complied, hopping his front feet onto the window,
and leaning in to plaster her face with his hand-towel sized
tongue.

it gives me a particular pleasure to see big greeted by our
neighbors.
pit bulls are supposed to be the terror of their neighborhood.
and there was a time when our neighbors were plenty wary of
my gentle giant.
his patience, and steady even temperament have made him so
many friends
that we cannot time our daily workouts any more.
we always have to stop for someone to pet the big.

now, if we were hanging out at the house,
big would gladly be petted until your arm fell off.
but the walk is important work,
so as soon as he had fulfilled his requested kiss,
he hopped down and pointed himself down the road, waiting
patiently.
as soon as i get done talking, the big is ready to move on.
the newspaper lady is doing her important work as well,
so we are all soon on our way again.

naresh got to see big on his game.
after the sun came up, naresh wanted to take some pictures.
first he dropped back to get a shot of us walking away.
big became very concerned.
the only thing naresh could capture was big looking back to see if
he was all right.
then naresh tried to get out front to photograph us coming
toward him.
he tried to outwit big by going all the way to the far side of the
road.

i could see the whites flashing,
as big cut his eyes to watch naresh
(it would be rude to stare)
and he picked up his pace to stay ahead.

big is the point man.
he is the one who spots the skunks and snakes.

he is the one who evaluates any strange dogs we meet.
naresh was out of his protective umbrella.

naresh got to see big resist the temptation,
as one short hare after another teased and tormented him.
at the end of the day he got to see big succumb,
as one short hare too many finally broke his resolve.
i could almost hear him, like popeye
(for those of you who remember the old popeye cartoons)
"i can't stands no more!"
and he was off.
then naresh got to see how to properly anchor a big.

actually, big and i have been thru this on our property,
where he is allowed to go without a leash,
and big will stop and come back immediately when i call him.
even in full pursuit he has always responded without hesitation.
but sometimes he reaches a breaking point and has to make that
first rush.
i have tried to explain to him;
"if you just don't look at them, big, it won't be so tempting."
but big is like the smoker who just wants to hold a cigarette in
his mouth...

"but i won't light it."
big has a prey response problem.

the one option we don't have is to go off leash when we leave the
farm. when you are a big, your life is at stake every time out.

naresh got to see big ignore barking dogs and curious cattle,
wild turkeys and squirrels.
and big got to see naresh as part of his responsibility.
once big has felt that you are in his care,
your place in the world changes.

when we got back to the porch,
the change in big's attitude was unmistakable.
naresh wanted a big kiss,
and big was more than happy to give him one...
or two, or three, or...
since we had finished work, there was no need to cut it short.

now, i am not going to count it as a done deal until the next visit.
but i know that big's aversion to men with sticks was pretty
profound.
but me, and dale, and ben, and other big team members carry
sticks
(this is loose dog country, and big isn't allowed to deal with
them, he just lets us know which ones are dangerous)
big doesn't bat an eye at our sticks.
i have a feeling that the next time we see naresh big will only
want to run to greet him.
i'd be willing to bet that the internal conflict is cured.

laz

07-05-12
the big rescue

so the heat wave continues, here in tennessee.
last week was brutal,
with low humidity,
made up for by highs anywhere from 105 to 114 degrees.
combined with the drought,
the effect on native species of plants and animals has been
devastating.
it looks like fall came early,
as trees are changing colors and dropping their leaves.
not the color change we expect in the fall,
with bright reds, oranges, and yellows.
the leaves dry out until they are crisp, while still green.
then they fade to yellow and white, or turn brown...
unless they fall off first.
the trees are sacrificing their leaves in a bid to simply survive.
some will and some won't.
no matter what happens now, this summer is over for the trees.

the corn crops are gone.
the leaves are long, narrow, and dried out.
most of the plants are dead where they stand.
what ears started forming before the severe weather hit
are thin and pitiful.
the going joke is that the only good thing is, the ears are already
roasted.

the only plant holding out any hope is the soybeans.
they are stunted, most not having grown in weeks.
a lot of the plants have died, and what is left is slowly dwindling.
but if the rains came back, the soybeans might make something.
unlike the native plants, the soybeans are engineered by man.
by happy coincidence, the soil in which these beans are bred to
thrive is shared with some of the western states where drought
resistance is always important.
so resistance to hot dry weather is part of their makeup.
the hardy soybean plants might be the last thing to completely
die.

our native plants have been engineered by nature for a water
rich environment.
some serious natural selection is taking place.

the animals have fared little better.
the porch fireplace, where amy, big, and myself dried ourselves
out during cold wet weather is not used during the summer.
even on spring nights when a fire might feel good on a chilly
evening, it sits idle.
we give it over as a nesting place for the declining chimney
swifts. like everyone else, we were pushed to put a cap on the
chimney to keep them out,
but we enjoy seeing them flit about in the mornings and
evenings.
we don't begrudge them the mosquitos and other bugs they eat.
and we don't find the chirping of the young,
as the parents come in and out with food,
to be irritating.
actually, i think it is pleasant.
and the only thing causing the swifts to decline...
is those darn chimney caps.
all they ask is a place to live.
that seems worth the minor inconvenience.

last week the afternoons outside were like something out of a
horror movie.
it looked like a normal summer woods
(except for the gradually increasing number of trees whose
leaves shriveled and burnt up in the sun)
but there was no sound.
not a bird, not an insect, not a lizard.
no barking dogs, no farm equipment in the distance.
not even a breath of wind.
nothing but total and complete silence.
nothing lived except the intolerable heat.

then the baby swifts started committing suicide.
the first one jumped while me & big were on the porch.
we heard a wet "plop" and looked over to see a naked baby bird
sprawled on the hearth.
big got there first,
and i really expected him to chomp it.

instead, he looked at the bird,
then at me with a worried expression on his face.
the bird gaped its mouth soundlessly a couple of times, and died.
when i picked it up, it was as hot as if it had come out of the oven.

big remained concerned.
even after the bird was gone.
he kept going back to where it had fallen,
sniffing around,
and then looking at me with the same worried expression.
me and big were equally helpless as the tally mounted.
there was nothing to do but wait on the weather to break.

we still heard the fluttering wings and chittering in the mornings,
as the parents continued to feed the surviving babies
until the heat became too extreme for even the bugs to be out.
one morning we came back from our walk just after daybreak
and found a living baby bird on the porch.
at first i thought it was dead,
but when big went over and sniffed at it,
sensing the presence it raised its head, mouth open,
and chirped out a demand for food.
i thought big would chomp it for sure,
but he just gave me that same worried look.
there is just no figuring out that dog.

attempts to start it back up the chimney were futile.
it was too young, and too weak.
but we put it in our ubiquitous small animal carrier,
and took it to a wildlife rehabilitator.
it has a lot of company, as the swifts are de-nesting in numbers
this summer.
big seemed satisfied that the bird left alive.
he didn't go thru the "mourning" process he did with the others.

for a couple of days, i thought that had been the last of the swifts.
then yesterday morning i heard the familiar fluttering,
followed by a frantic chirping.
somehow, the hardiest of the hardy was still hanging in there.

this morning after we came back from the walk,
me and big were spending our quality time on the porch.
but big was distracted.

he kept walking over to the fireplace,
looking at me,
and then coming back over to me.
"are you still upset about the baby birds, big fella?"

i got him to hang around briefly for some petting,
but big was pretty determined about going to look at the
fireplace.
finally i went over there to look with him...

and saw what he was all tore up about.
the last baby had come down the chimney,
and was hanging from the side of a cardboard box sitting on the
hearth.
this baby was much stronger than the previous one.
i looked up the chimney and could see the nest about halfway up.
it looked empty now.
and the walls of the chimney were too slick for it to have a
chance of climbing up.
however, there was a small ledge a little ways up.
i reached up with him,
gave him a chance,
and he clung to the ledge without difficulty.
me & big discussed our options.
"he's better off if his parents raise him, big guy."
big looked wise.
"he's pretty far down, but there aren't any other babies. maybe
they'll find him."
big thought it best to simply continue looking wise.

we hung out on the porch to see if we could tell what happened.
big isn't the best at patience.
he kept wanting to go look up the chimney,
to see if the bird was still on the ledge.
"the parents aren't coming down, if they see your ugly face
looking up, big guy."

i called him back,
and he struggled with starting over to check on his bird,
and then coming back, because he wasn't supposed to look up
the chimney.
he needed more than a few reminders.

he really needed a reminder when we heard the fluttering,
and the baby began chirruping like mad.
"big, we can't look to see. he's too close."
we waited until we'd heard it several times.
there were no longer any other babies calling, except the one.

i was like big,
i wanted to peek around the corner so bad.
but the only way we'll know if the bird is actually getting fed
is tomorrow morning when his cries will either be stronger or
weaker.
i suppose there would be still time for another trip to the
rehabilitator's place, if need be.

one thing for sure, i can't let him die.
big would be terribly disappointed.
add another facet to the surprising big dog.
he runs the big bird rescue.

laz

07-08-12
the big rain

once the humidity came back it was just a matter of time.
put that much moisture, and that much heat, in the air
and thunderstorms are bound to result.

not that it didn't get even more miserable before things finally
broke at the big farm.

for a couple of days, the afternoon clouded up,
thunder and lightning were all around,
and what showers fell, fell on someone else.

yesterday it finally came our turn.
we had gotten too jaded by the disappointments to get excited
when it clouded up.
we didn't bat an eye when we heard the thunder.
but suddenly it was pouring rain...

it only lasted 15 or 20 seconds, but it was rain.
after another half hour of scattered sprinkles,
we got a second downpour.
this one had to last close to 5 minutes.
it wasn't the soaking rain we need,
but it was a relief.
and it was enough to settle the dust and wet the ground.
unfortunately, it didn't bring any cool air down with it,
so last night was a tennessee muggy special.

during the heat wave, even big has changed his style.
i've been getting up extra early so we can finish the walk shortly
after sunup.
he still hears my eyes open,
but he doesn't come roaring out demanding that i hurry.
he just goes to the end of his cable and waits...panting.
as long as i stay on schedule, he doesn't make a peep.
if i change from my set routine,
by so much as forgetting my shoes and making an extra trip to
the bedroom,
then he barks.
that dog knows everything that happens in the house.

and he has a clear picture of what *should* be happening,
and in what order.

i still get an emotional "wooo wooo wooo" when i come around
the corner with his leash,
but the jumping is pretty subdued...
altho i got a halfsized flip the day i forgot my shoes.

there isn't much need to settle him down at the start.
it is already hot, and our walks show it.
we just never cut one short.
i wonder; if i could read big's pee-mails,
is he telling the other dogs he wishes we'd get a rainout?
"master must really love his walks. and i can't let him go alone.
but this is killing me!"

this morning was extra special.
the dew point has been steadily climbing,
but the low temps have been staying above it.
this morning the two must have nearly converged.
the air was so heavy with water,
i suspected drops would fall if i shouted.

the whippoorwills were still sounding when we headed down
the driveway,
but as the twilight steadily grew,
they were soon joined by the sounds of the surviving songbirds.
yesterday's rain must have renewed their hopes as well.

a little later i heard crows over on mr brothers' hills.
those wouldn't be our short creek crows.
they held on to what they had during the battle in the big woods,
but haven't recovered any territory since.
a little later, passing ben & susan's place,
we arrived just as the short creek murder came out for the day.

the main band of three came out in a raucously cawing group.
the fourth came out cawing shortly behind them.
then there was a long gap,
as i wondered if they had lost another member,
before the laggard came out flapping furiously,
and cawing for everyone else to wait.

every time we see them, one crow is way behind the rest.
i asked big if he thinks it is always the same one.
big looked at me wisely, and kept his counsel.
big knows how to look even smarter by saying nothing.

we caught back up with the short creek crows down at ben's
soybean fields.
they were foraging noisily, as always.
one of them always in a tree by the creek,
keeping an eye out for our local hawk.
it was still too early for the hawk,
he never comes out till the sun is up.
but there are still bobcats and coyotes to look out for,
or maybe even a man with a gun
(who might take a potshot at a crow just for the heck of it)
diligence and teamwork are mandatory, if crows want to survive.

there has only been one hawk this summer,
and he has been roosting in different places.
me & big don't think there is a nest this year.
he has been circling over our heads on our return trip lately;
screeing a greeting...

and probably watching for any short hares that big might flush.
whatever his real motive, we pretend he is welcoming us back.

we don't know if there is any more food for the crows to find this
morning, but they seem to be having a great time.
rain has never been welcomed with more enthusiasm than here
at short creek.

even tho it was too dark to see clearly,
it seemed like the little soybean sprouts have perked up.
i told big we would know for sure on the way home.
we were coming back the same way.

as we walked along, the wet roads turned to patchy wet.
finally we walked out of the rained on area altogether.
by the time we got to millersburg, it was bone dry.

the sun came up on the way home,
and the first rays took the life out of us.
as we got back into the rain territory,

things only got worse.
the road was drying out as soon as the first sun touched it.
if there was 100% humidity when we started,
it must have climbed to 120% before we got home.

big walked like we were on the 4th day of a 6-day race.
there in the sun, the soybeans were happy with the humidity.
they really had perked up overnight.
the native plants presented a more mixed bag.
a lot of trees and other plants,
which had appeared wilted beyond salvation,
were showing varying degrees of fighting back.
but the dead stuff was still dead.

according to the weather, we are supposed to get real rain
tomorrow and monday.
if it comes, it will be educational to see how things recover.
except the soybeans.
if we get a good rain,
the hardy soybeans will make something.
it will be late (they have lost weeks of growth)
but they will make something.

by the time we turned up the driveway,
big and i were both ready to get home.
big was huffing and puffing,
i was soaked.
i could even feel sweat beading up in my moustache.

i have been letting big ride out the worst of the heat in the
garage.
after the first day, when he didn't know where we were going,
all i have to do is ask big;
"do you want to go in the garage & get out of this heat?"
he wags his eager agreement,
and then i let him off the cable.
he waits around each corner of the house,
until he sees that i am coming,
and when i get to the garage door,
he will be sitting there, tail wagging, waiting to be let in.

this morning, as is our custom,
i let big off the leash when we got to the farm,

just like always he walked alongside me.
but when we got to the top of the drive,
instead of heading for the back porch where his food was waiting,
big went straight to the garage door, and looked back at me.
i had to laugh at the hopeful expression on his face.
"naw, big guy, not right now. we need to do breakfast first, and then you can go to the garage."
big didn't eat anything until supper.

i am sure hoping that rain comes in like they promised.
a real rain, enough to cool things off.
somehow i suspect big hopes for it even more.

laz

07-10-12
the big chimney swift mystery

i will be the first to say that the big has challenged much of what i
have learned about dogs.
many an entrenched belief has gone by the wayside...

starting with that day at the beginning of the big saga,
when i stated with confidence;
"i can build a pen that will hold him. he is only a dog, and i am
smarter than any dog!"

one thing, tho, has been reliable.
big is a terrier.
a giant terrier, maybe a genius terrier,
but a terrier none the less.
and terriers were created for one purpose.
they kill small animals.

this does not make them bad dogs,
but for countless generations their prey response has been
emphasized to the nth degree.
no matter what the training,
or the temperament,
no one who understands dogs would ever leave a terrier alone
with a small animal.

for all big's remarkable abilities,
his greatest challenges revolve around his prey response.
i haven't attempted to change big's nature with his training,
it has all been about developing the discipline to control his
impulses when he is "on the job."
and he does quite well.
not perfect, but he is pretty good.

against this backdrop,
big's attachment to the chimney swifts is a complete mystery to
me.
it isn't like he is fond of birds.
he doesn't harbor any secret affection for buzzards or turkeys.
when a foolish mockingbird came within his reach,
the result was lightning quick and predictable.

he didn't share his food with the little pellet snatching nuthatch...
at least not willingly.
and he didn't show any interest in the swifts,
until the first kamikaze chick came plummeting down the
chimney.
as soon as he categorized the noisy feedings as just a sound that
comes from the chimney,
he paid it little mind...

until that first baby landed in the fireplace with a plop.
the big guy was clearly distressed by the dead chick.

his lassie act with the first live jumper was still a surprise.
he seemed to be relieved when i took it away
(and "fixed" the problem)

last week we had a second live jumper.
this one was older, black tipping the feathers on its wings and
tail.
it was able to make it's own way back up the chimney,
once i gave it a boost up to the ledge around the damper.

last night it came down again.
i wouldn't have known,
except big started the lassie act again this morning,
while we were getting ready to walk.
i forgot my trainer, and we came up on the porch to get it.
big was instantly aware of the bird,
going back and forth,
leading me to spot a 4 inch black circle on the outside of the
chimney,
barely visible in the first beginnings of light.
it was big's baby swift, now fully feathered.

big seemed satisfied when i boosted it up to the ledge,
and we went for our walk.

the first thing he did when we returned
was to go look up the chimney.
the swift was gone, now able to quickly climb back up where it
belonged.

now he hurries over to the chimney every time we hear the
fluttering and chirruping.
he puts his front feet on the hearth,
and looks up the chimney,
cocking his ears and turning his head from side to side.
big fusses over his baby swift like an anxious mother,
and i am at a loss to explain it.

i have heard of nursing mother dogs adopting other animals.
but big is no mother.
and he has never distinguished himself as the protector of small
defenseless animals...
until now.
i cannot think of an explanation for his behavior,
except big has an affection for those baby chimney swifts.

hardly qualifying as an expert on dog behavior,
i am open to any reasonable alternative?

laz

07-10-12
the big picture

i apologize for the flurry of big posts.
but i have to get them in now.
when carl arrives, we launch into the as yet unknown adventures of the vol-state,
big posts will be out of your hair (and inbox) for at least a couple of weeks.

and poor big.
the vol-state is not his best time of year.
too many days i will not be around.
no walk, no master.
all my fun will be tainted by the memory of my loyal companion...
alone at home, waiting for me to return.

and he won't be greeting me with recriminations over his abandonment,
but with pure unfettered joy.
because that is the way of the bigs.
i will feel guilty anyway.

at least he got to go into his personal vol-state hell off a glorious series of days.

with big books 2 & 3 making their slow way thru publishing,
we wanted to add a little something.
a section of pictures of big and his friends and neighbors.
pictures of the roads and trails and the hills where he lives.
so we have been having big picture days.

big is one tough customer to photograph.
with a mystical ability to detect cameras,
he is determined not to co-operate.
that resolve wavered when he found himself with visitors,
and extra walks that were not even on his schedule.

naresh came down over the weekend to take a lot of the pictures.
we had wondered how big would respond to the next naresh visit...
now that naresh was part of the big team.

well...
his first response was even greater conflict.
when he heard naresh, he came running out to greet him,
tail wagging.
but as naresh got close his big nerve broke.
he backed away, barking a warning for naresh not to try
anything funny.
but his tail kept on wagging.
his heart and his head were sending different messages.

the conflict ended when naresh & i came out with the leash.
if it means a walk, big is all in.
from then on, naresh was a-ok as far as big was concerned.

big had hardly started his post-walk nap when we came back
with his leash.
when we headed out on the trails, big was elated.
we don't do many trails in chigger and rattlesnake season.
he took his position as rattlesnake scout with pleasure
and followed the trails as flawlessly as ever.
big has a phenomenal memory of places.

it was a very confusing walk.
naresh trailed on the way out,
and periodically we would turn and walk back towards naresh.

when we jumped a fallen tree,
and then turned and jumped it the other way,
big looked at me like i had lost my mind.
"why the heck didn't we just stay on this side?"
big couldn't understand our seemingly purposeless walk.
walks are supposed to *go somewhere!*

when we ignored big's suggestion to take a left at the last turn,
big lost his motivation.
heading home with trails left unpatrolled made no sense.
big never wants to turn for home.
we had to urge him all the way up the hill.

once we got to the house,
the steaming hot big went straight for his pool.
that suited our needs perfectly,
as we wanted a picture of big splashing.

however, big just stood in the water and looked at us.
there is a reason no one had yet caught his splashing on camera.
but we had a plan.
i might not be absolutely smarter than big,
but i can win a round now and then.
we told big bye, and went to the house.
we went thru the house and peered at big thru the window.
the big guy was watching where we had disappeared on the back
porch.
satisfied we were gone, he got back in the pool.
naresh lined the camera up thru the window.

then big turned and looked right at us.
catching naresh in the window, he got back out of the pool.
naresh threw his hands up and turned away...
but i kept watching, hidden around the corner in the shadows.

sure enough, big saw naresh leave, got back in the pool,
and started splashing away.
as soon as he turned his head away i whispered to naresh;
"come now, quick!"
we got several pictures without mr big suspecting a thing.

after big had time to cool down,
we came out with his leash again.
by this time it was blazing hot,
but the big is always game.
we planned to walk down to ben and susan's and get some
pictures with susan and the girls.
big was suffering so much by the time we got to the road
that we had no heart for making him go on,
so we returned to the house,
susan, laura kate, and anna grace came over
and sat on the front porch with big for much of the afternoon.
naresh was snapping away,
but big wasn't about to mess with such a happy setup.
three people petting him at once?
life doesn't get better than that.

before the day was over, even sandra had sat with the big for a
session of photos and petting.

it was the best day the big dog ever had.

we had one final photo shoot this morning.
ben had been out of town before,
and we hadn't got any pictures of ben and susan's farm because
of the heat.
so ben called last night and said he was running at 6:15,
and would meet me at the end of his driveway.
susan would take the pictures.

sandra said;
"6:15? why not 6, or a little after 6?"
i told her;
"because it is ben."
you have to know ben.

i couldn't sleep past 4:30,
and once big heard my eyes open the clock was running.
when i still hadn't made an appearance by 5, he started barking.
so i went out with no leash and asked him if he wanted to sit on
the porch for a while?
it is a luxury to have a dog that understands english.
big went on up to the porch, and we had about an hour to talk,
pet, and listen to the swifts start their day.

being sneaky, i had put the leash in my chair.
big checked up on the table for it,
but it wasn't there, so he relaxed.
i fooled him! i was sitting on it.
when i pulled it out from under my butt, he leapt to his feet,
ready to go.

if ben is punctual, i am early.
we timed it out to reach the end of his drive precisely 5 minutes
early.
i think you have to be a runner to understand how it is possible
to know exactly how far everything is,
and precisely how long it takes to get there.
at 6:15...
not 6:14, and not 6:16...
we saw ben's door open, and ben came out running,
buddy tight on his heels.
watching ben run down the hill from his house, i marveled at
how smooth he looked.

ben is the undisputed top runner in short creek.
from fosterville to millersburg, he has no peer.
i was jealous of his effortless stride.
then he crossed the creek halfway down his driveway,
and started uphill.
watching him labor up the hill to the gate brought a smile to my face.
i wasn't near as jealous of that part.
ben is a downhiller at heart.

about that time, i saw susan pull out in her van.
they would reach the gate at about the same time.

it was a perfect morning for a photo shoot.
dawn light just breaking, and the fields and hills swathed in mist.
and the meeting between me & big and ben & buddy is a regular occurrence.
ben always runs the same route. at the same time.
any time me & big do that route,
or one that crosses it,
i can set my watch by when and where we meet ben.
buddy lags behind something terrible.
he falls way back, then cuts across a field, or thru the woods to catch up.
then repeats.

the last mile and a half he has no chance to take a shortcut.
when me & big meet ben almost to the end of his loop,
we know we will meet the struggling buddy about 10 minutes later.

whenever we meet, ben stops to talk
(stopping his watch so his time isn't messed up)
whenever buddy catches up, he and big act socially awkward.
they get along fine,
but big always tries too hard with other dogs.
he may be smooth with the ladies, but he is clumsy around dogs.

this morning had a different dynamic.
ben has generally petted big before buddy gets there.
seeing ben pet big is acceptable, more or less.
but buddy did not like it when big acted familiar with susan.
he got right up in big's face and growled.

big might be terrified of bicycles, and afraid of dark-skinned men,
but he is not afraid of dogs.
his hackles stood up and he growled right back.
ben and susan were simultaneously surprised...
"was that buddy that growled?"

i didn't have time to explain.
this was not my idea of a good situation.
buddy wasn't leashed,
and i wasn't in a position where i could use the trainer to keep
some space.
all i could do was watch what was happening and react.
this one was big's to handle.

the return growl seemed to set buddy back,
but the two dogs sort of jostled around until they were side by
side, looking at each other.
i was trying to figure out what to do if a fight started.

buddy looks like a lot larger dog,
but he wouldn't be capable of inflicting the damage on big,
that big could inflict on him.
i sure did wish buddy was on a leash.
then buddy did a shoulder bump.
i was caught by surprise.
maybe i shouldn't have been.
most animals try to settle disputes with contests of size or
strength, rather than violence.
but i had never heard of the shoulder bump until i saw big do it
to little.

big has done it to little a lot.
(little can be a pain in the butt)
i could have warned buddy how that would work for him.
i have tried to move big when he is set.
buddy might be a lot taller dog
(not necessarily an advantage in terms of leverage)
but big is a block.
buddy's shoulder bump didn't move big an inch.
but the return shoulder bump
(which big has practiced plenty with little)
raised both buddy's front feet off the ground, and knocked him

back a foot.
the situation defused rapidly from there.
buddy gave ground,
altho he stayed between big and ben as much as possible.
he didn't growl again, except when there was plenty of space
between him and big.
big would raise his hackles a little, but otherwise ignored buddy.
i relaxed as it became obvious that everyone understood their
relative place.
big is not a fighter; the way you can not be a fighter when you
don't have anything to prove.

susan took a lot of pictures of me & ben, buddy & big.
ben & big, me & big, and all combinations in between.
the farm should be featured well in the backgrounds.
but i will be curious to see if any of them capture those first
interactions between the dogs.

there is a lot that goes on with them,
that you only see if you are watching.

laz

07-26-12
facebook hell

we are all idiots about some things.

the facebook phenomenon has always been a mystery to me.
when it first started, i thought it was just something teenagers
would do.
eventually they would tire of it and move on with real life.

as with so many things in this world, i was completely wrong.
facebook seemed to acquire a life of its own,
sucking in everyone.
i saw the women at work "facebooking" and could not
understand the appeal.
they sat there, rapt, scrolling thru what looked like just endless
crap.
i even asked; trying to understand just what was going on.

"you can keep up with your friends"
"you can reconnect with old acquaintances"
"you can let people know what you are up to"

this made things no clearer.
people have hundreds of "facebook friends"
how can you possibly want to know what 289 people are doing?
i supposed it was made easier by the fact that what those 289
people were probably doing was looking at facebook.
i didn't feel the need to "reconnect"
those people have probably purged me from their memories, and
don't want to be reminded.
besides, what if they still bear a grudge?
and who the heck would want to know what i am "up to?"
my life would make boring reading.
i do my miles, i work on the farm, i watch judge judy.

and so i have breezed thru the age of facebook;
happily faceless, smug in the knowledge that i had so much extra
time to actually do things.

and then came vol-state 2012.

i didn't get to tell sandra hardly anything that happened.
she already knew.
"it's all over facebook."

i grew antsy while waiting on the race reports to come in.
the one i saw only served to whet my appetite for more.
vol-state race reports are always fascinating reading.
i wouldn't tell sandra
(she would revel in knowing things i didn't know)
but i got more and more curious
about what it was that was "all over facebook."
i soon discovered that i couldn't find anything on facebook.
i was not a member.

i should have known better.
but we are all idiots about some things.
"what could it hurt?" i asked myself.
"i will just make an account and put nothing on it."
"i won't ever have to look at it again, but i will be able to see what
it is that is 'all over facebook.'"
did i mention that we are all idiots about some things?

i was honestly surprised how little information i was required to
give.
it wanted my e-mail.
then it insisted on getting my birthdate, mentioning something
about "age appropriate content."
my pulse quickened, as i imagined there must be nudity on
facebook.
maybe i should have done this a long time ago!

i didn't realize it at the time, but this would be the high water
mark of my facebook experience.

then i came to a page that cheerfully announced;
"you may already know these people"
there was a column of tiny pictures, and to my complete
surprise...
i did know those people!

next to each tiny picture was a little box for me to click if i
wanted to be "facebook friends" with those people.
that made little sense, as i could not see why they would want to

see a blank page.
and if they endeavored to contact me there...
i would never know it.
besides, the term "facebook friends" just sounds creepy.

while i was pondering how facebook knew i might know those
people, more of them appended to the list.
i scrolled down to see them, and again;
some i knew, some i didn't know, but they all seemed to have
some connection with ultra-running.
some of them were big names in the sport,
people i doubted would have any interest in being my "facebook
friend."
there were also a number of cute young girls, who i didn't know.
i clicked on a couple of their tiny pictures, wondering if this was
the nudity implied when i entered my birth date.
it wasn't, and one of them even came back and told me it was
"private"...

making me feel like a stalker.
it has taken a lot of wear and tear to reach the stage in life where
cute girls treat me like a harmless old man,
instead of acting like i "creep them out."
i was glad i had chosen not to click the facebook friend boxes.

this went on for quite a while.
as soon as i looked at one group of pictures, another appended
on the bottom.
it finally got so long that my computer locked up,
and i had to reboot.
my hard drive (made of baked clay, inscribed with a sharp reed)
just wasn't up to the task.

after i rebooted my computer, facebook was waiting in my e-
mail.
it accusingly told me i had one more step to join facebook.
i completed the process and set about trying to find what was
"all over facebook."

i was unable to find anything.
heck, i didn't even know how to find my own facebook page.
i tried to recall what sandra had told me when she explained
facebook.

all i could remember was that when something was on someone
else's facebook page,
it was on hers as well,
and a lot of stuff about being private and something about a
timeline.
to be honest, every time she started explaining facebook to me it
quickly faded into a sort of droning background noise,
while i nodded once in a while and my mind wandered.
i think this is a natural skill that is embedded in the "why?"
chromosome.
it might have been helpful if i had listened...

but i will never know that for sure.

i just chalked the whole thing up as an experiment failed,
and considered my foray into facebook as being at an end...

how wrong i was.
my facebook hell was only beginning.

when i re-opened my e-mail, there was a message from facebook.
"tim e" wanted to be my facebook friend.
he even sent a tiny picture,
i suppose in case i had forgotten what he would look like
if he was on a postage stamp.
i wondered how the heck he knew about my facebook "page"
(the blank one i don't even know how to find)
i finally decided it must have been pure random chance.
i wasn't sure what to do.
clicking the friend box would be a bad response.
he might expect me to be able to access facebook.
if he tried to facebook me, he would think i was an jerk.
but then, if i ignore his request...
i suppose he would think i was an jerk.
maybe i could send him an e-mail, and tell him it was all a
horrible mistake....

this seemed like a good plan,
so i went back to my e-mail....

only to find 4 more friend requests.
i could feel my chest getting tight, i was trapped, and a little
panicked.

as i stared helplessly at the screen another one popped up.
this was worse than the nightmare of christmas cards.
i turned off my computer and went to bed.

it was with a sense of dread that i turned it on the next morning.
my worst fears were realized,
those requests had proliferated thruout the night.
i wasn't sure what had happened.
maybe facebook had sent out some sort of general notice;
"a moron has attempted to join us. act now and we can break his spirit."

i tried to look at a few of them.
i wasn't sure what i would do,
but i wasn't brave enough to click any friend boxes.
i was already in over my head.
i thought maybe i could destroy my facebook page.
except i couldn't even find it.
i looked at the requests, hoping for some sort of clue what to do.
unfortunately i couldn't find the choice;
"i apologize, but i have no stinking idea what i am doing and am afraid to make you my friend."

when i came to the one where a slightly deranged looking joe lugiano was glaring at me accusingly from his postage stamp, my spirit was broken.
okay, he might not look slightly deranged.
i can't really see those tiny pictures very well.
but i am sure he was glaring at me accusingly.
i turned off my computer.

unfortunately, turning off my computer is not helping anything.
every time i turn it back on, there are more.
i am carefully saving them all unanswered until i figure out what to do.
i can't ask sandra.
she will think i am an idiot...

actually, she already thinks i am an idiot.
but i don't want to confirm it.
i don't think she gets that we are all idiots about some things.

i am in facebook hell.
and there wasn't even any nudity!

if you are not in facebook hell, take it from me.
if you stumble onto the place to join,
reboot your computer immediately...

and never go back.

laz

07-27-12
the big vol-state

they also serve, who only stand and wait.
(milton)

everyone knew the vol-state was going to involve some suffering.
everyone, that is, except big.
the runners faced the physical and mental challenges of running
500 kilometers.
blisters, fatigue, heat, rain, sleep deprivation, hunger, and thirst
were (at a minimum) their challenges.
carl, naresh, and myself, as race officials,
faced the challenges of riding herd over a field of runners that
would ultimately string out over more than 100 miles.
sleepless nights and countless miles of driving, missed meals and
exposure to the elements;
our discomfort was minimal compared to the pain endured by
the runners...
but it was not inconsequential.
the families; spouses and children also made sacrifices.
missing their loved one,
worrying that they were in trouble, or in pain.
(altho most spouses eventually figure that the runner brought
the pain on themselves, so "too bad, too sad")

but no one would have it worse than the big.
big didn't get a choice, and he didn't know what was coming...

or when it would end,

with amy off living the high life in cape cod,
there was no one who could replace any part of his routine.
sandra would cope with him the best she could, but big was
going to be a very sad dog.

i did my best to minimize the disruption for big.
we left tuesday night, instead of wednesday morning.
part of the reason was to get more sleep before the early meeting
at the finish to load the runners on a bus to ride to the start.
we'd have had to leave the house about 2am.
the other part was that big accepts people leaving in the evening.

leave in the morning, without going for his walk, and big is one
unhappy dog.
his walk is his job, and his job is his life.
big is a working dog.

there was a time that big was disconsolate if i left for even a day.
he wouldn't eat or sleep, but would only mourn my absence.
over time he came to accept that i might be gone for a day or two,
but i would always come home.
if i was not home, he would accept missing a walk or two.
big knows everything that happens in the house,
including who is home.

the race did not pass close enough to the house for us to return
home until sunday.
that was well over big's limit.
he had begun to employ all his means of peaceful protest.
he started pushing his bigloo out in the middle of the yard.
sandra could barely push it back.
he repeatedly let himself off his cable, and came up on the porch.
he would go back when she asked,
but later let himself off again.

we came in late sunday,
and the first thing i heard was big's frantic call for me to come
out and see him.
when i came around the corner his "help me" bark morphed into
his loving "wooo wooo wooo."
walking out in the darkness, i could hear long silences
punctuated by his feet hitting the ground with a thud.
he must be performing the gamut of leaps and flips in his
repertoire.
i regretted that i couldn't see it,
judging by the gaps between thuds he had to be getting some
impressive air time.

as soon as i got within reach, the big fella wrapped himself
around my legs like a plaster cast.
as i petted and talked to him i could feel his whole body shake
with his wagging tail.
this was one desperately lonely dog.
i had only intended to pet him a few minutes,

then catch some sleep so we could walk before i left in the morning.
i didn't have the heart to cut him short.
i let him off his cable and we went up on the porch for about an hour.
he wallered and rolled about, intent on touching me with every square inch of his skin
(and there are a lot of square inches of skin on a big)
he leaned back into my lap and looked up into my eyes with the saddest look i ever saw.
his eyes were like lasers cutting me to the heart.
i didn't even want to think about being gone for another week.

after i finally went to bed, we got hit with a monster thunderstorm.
big didn't care.
he pushed his bigloo out into the middle of the yard and stood in the rain in protest.
when i didn't show up by first light,
he took off his cable and came up on the porch to get me.

big and i walked out into the dwindling raindrops as the storm ended.
he was exquisitely happy, and on his best behavior.
all through our morning routine, the big was a perfect gentleman...

but when carl and i got back in the van he protested loudly.
i felt sorry for sandra, trying to keep him happy for the next week.

part of managing the vol-state is dealing with the extended parade of runners.
another part is like the age old riddles of crossing rivers with various boats and loads.
shuffling vehicles around when the number of drivers and vehicles don't match can get pretty complicated.
as we left monday morning, i dropped carl off to pick up his van in war trace.
then i continued on the course,
while carl returned to the house to pick up some supplies he had left stashed during the first half of the race.

carl no sooner started to load than who would show up but the
big. he had let himself off the cable and ran to get in the van.
wherever carl was going, he must have figured i would be there
as well.
as far as big was concerned, he belonged with me.
none the less, he obediently followed carl back to his cable...

only to show up back in the van a few minutes later.
big was desperate.

all thru the week i worried about my big friend.
sandra's reports were less than encouraging.
pushing his bigloo all over the yard,
strewing his bedding in the mud,
letting himself loose repeatedly.
big was a most unhappy dog.
my greatest fear was that he would decide to go and look for me.
big is safe up on the hill.
he is fairly safe in the neighborhood.
but if he wanders far from home at all, he becomes a target.
he is a gentle giant in a hostile world.

finally, saturday, i got my chance.
we had a long enough gap between finishers to make a run to the
house and pick up my partner.
the last finisher should be early enough that we could take him
home afterwards.
naresh and i made the hurried trip from the rock to the big farm
and back.
big was tickled to be with us.
he loved the vehicle; unlike my non-air-conditioned vehicles, this
one was cool on a hot day.
best of all, he could sit with his head resting on the console
between naresh and i, and have an air-conditioning vent playing
directly on his broad chest.

up on the rock, big was the happiest dog on earth.
he got petted.
he schmoozed with the ladies
(and he *is* the ladies man that he thinks he is)
some small measure of his 2 weeks of hell was repaid out in the
woods.

unfortunately, the last finisher that day did not come in when expected.
we were stuck holing up in a motel while we waited,
and big did not enjoy that one bit.
my big guy is a country dog, not a city dog.
this dog that can hear my eyes open inside the house was overwhelmed by sound.
constant traffic on the interstate, horns honking,
jack brakes blasting, loud trucks and motorbikes;
it all combined to put big on edge.

it was all complicated by the need for secrecy.
some motels allow pets.
none allow bigs.
we had to keep him hidden not only from motel personnel,
but from our fellow guests.
and we had to keep him from barking.

fortunately, big is a well behaved dog.
i was able to slip him out unnoticed for a couple of trips behind the motel.
the two times he let loose a single bark, he immediately quieted on command.
when i went outside, he lay in front of the door and stared at the crack nonstop...
until i returned.
he was very worried about getting left behind in this scary place.
he was relieved when we got back in the van to go out for the last finisher.
he loved being back in the woods.
but afterwards it was too late to drive home.
it wasn't that i had too little sleep.
i don't need much.
but i hadn't slept at the same time on consecutive days in over a week.
48 hour stretches without sleep,
followed by two 1 hour naps in an 8 hour period.
sleeping in the day, the evening, or the early morning, as the opportunity arose.
i had the ultimate case of jet lag.
driving back to kimball i knew only a fool would try to drive home without some rest.

big was stuck with a night in the motel.
naresh was out like a light within minutes.
big lay between the beds with his head on his paws.
when i looked down, he was looking back at me.
his eyes begged to go home to his bigloo in the woods.
he wanted to listen to katydids and whippoorwills, not trucks
and radios.
when i woke a few hours later, he hadn't moved.
his eyes met mine with the same begging look.
i wondered if he had slept at all.

we went for a walk while naresh finished his beauty sleep.
big begged to get in the van as we left,
and he couldn't wait to get back...

begging to get in the van again as we returned to the room.
no one was happier than big when we finally got on the road.
back at home i promised him;
"it is all over big guy. we are back on schedule."
i was as good as my word, coming out to get him before sunup
the next morning.
i know my way in the dark as well as any blind person.
when i got to big, i could tell that he had wrapped his cable
around the hackberry tree.
sometimes he does that in the morning when he comes to meet
me for his walk.
and we have a routine for it.
i tell him;
"we gotta go back around the tree, mr big."
then we walk together to the tree,
whereupon big takes off running around it and back to where i
hook him to his leash...
and i jump around the tree to avoid being cut down by his cable.

this morning big didn't feel like waiting.
when i told him;
"we gotta go back around the tree, mr big."
he took off running.
i felt the cable hit the back of my heel;
in the darkness i had stepped inside it.

i tried to jump, and cleared one foot.
but his cable quickly tightened around the other ankle,
and jerked me off my feet.
as i fell, i yelled out;
"STOP!"
big stopped on a dime.
one more step and he'd have been dragging me,
the cable cutting into my flesh.
"STOP!" has turned out to be an invaluable skill for my big friend.

i disentangled my leg and told big "OK" as i got to my feet.
he ran on around the tree and out to the end of his cable,
then he sat down to wait on me to come attach his big blue leash.

we had a wonderful walk that morning.
we watched the clouds turn pink, and then watched the sun
come up.
we saw white-tail deer and short hares.
we stopped to admire this year's baby donkey.
once it got light i had a chance to survey our home territory
and check out how it was rebounding from the drought,
after two weeks of rain.
but that is another story altogether.
the important thing for big was that his vol-state ordeal was
over.

laz

07-27-12
the big secret

caught him!

one of big's mysteries has been his technique for removing his
"dogproof" collar.
we know he can take it off almost at will,
but the big guy is pretty close with his secrets.
all this time, we have never caught him in the act.

the way the collar works is that it has two loops,
a big loop and a small loop.
the larger one goes around the neck, the smaller one is empty.
the cable attachment is on the empty loop.
the collar itself can slip thru a ring between the two loops,
so any pulling on it at all causes it to slip thru the ring making the
empty loop larger, and making the other part tighten around his
neck. it is a clever and effective design.
as advertised, a dog cannot "back out" of it.
dogproof it may be.
bigproof it is not.

this morning mr brothers was over looking at places to dump a
load of dirt (to fill those flower beds i have been building)
we did go out and pet the big a little.
he thinks mr brothers is part of his team, and was anxious to
properly greet him.

apparently the amount of petting was inadequate.
we were standing next to the back porch talking.
big was at the end of his cable, wagging his tail and watching us.

out of the corner of my eye, i saw him step back from the end of
his cable.
suddenly he spun around, sticking his front foot into the collar,
dropped his head upside down, with his nose pointing back
towards his tail.
there was a sudden jerk
(the details of which were too fast for me to see)
and the collar was flying thru the air back into the middle of his
area.

the now free big came flying,
that look of unbridled joy on his face,
and sat down between us like he was just one of the guys.
we looked at big.
big looked from one of us to the other...
and grinned.

after a few moments i told him;
"go get on the porch."
two giant bounds and he was on the porch.
he turned around and faced us.
"now sit down and wait."
big sat, and looked at us expectantly.
when we started towards mr brothers' truck,
big stood up.
"you sit back down and stay there."
big sat back down.

when he heard mr brothers open the truck door,
big came flying.
orders or no orders,
he is not going to let me leave him again any time soon.
he looked at mr brothers,
then ran around and looked at the passenger door, then at me...
grinning.
"we aren't going anywhere bigness. now go get back on the
porch where you belong."
off around the corner he shot, still running at big speed.
i heard his feet hit on the landing, then on the porch.

that big. what a goobus. i didn't have to see him to know he was
sitting at the top of the steps, and craning his neck trying to see
around the corner of the house.

i might not have the details down,
especially in that jerk that releases the collar.
but i have a good idea now, just how he gets it off.
what else would you expect,
after all, i am the human,
and not about to be outsmarted by some mere dog.
that's why i am in charge!

laz

07-29-12
another big day

there are a lot of different ways to watch the sun come up.
me & big have tried them all during our early morning workouts.
most people only think about sunrise as something to watch
head on, but watching sunrise with the sun behind gives a whole
different perspective.

it was still dark as i hooked up coach big and we headed out.
somewhere out in the woods an owl hooo-hooo-hoooted,
and i wondered if it was answering big's wooo-wooo-wooo
greeting when i came out to get him.

for once it wasn't already stifling hot.
for the first time in the whole of july,
the temperature had dipped below 70 during the night.
i could feel big's joy when i petted him a moment before
attaching his leash.
it doesn't seem possible that any dog could be happier than big
when we work out,
but he seems to always have another gear...
another higher gear.
i don't know what to call this gear.
what is the next step up from ebullient?

anyway, as we make our way down the driveway
the first lightening of the predawn twilight reveals a prancing
coach big
dancing around just shy of the end of his leash.
i am relieved that he has the physical control to prance without
pulling.
i got caught up in working on my flowerbeds yesterday
and am pretty sore from overdoing it.
big always seems to know what is up,
and this day he won't end up pulling at all.

"lets do fosterville road today, mr big."
"don't you think it will be fun to watch the sun come up from
behind? "
while we watched the world emerge from the darkness

we talked about the transformation that had happened during
the vol-state.
after 2 months of drought and extreme heat had left everything
brown and apparently dead,
the vol-state had brought two weeks of rain.
steady rains, pouring rains, and torrential thunderstorms had
begun when the race started,
and the final thunderstorm had brewed up 11 days later when
the final finisher was reaching the finish.
as the outlines of the hills began to appear, we could see the
recovery in process.
many of the trees, notably the sycamore and hackberry, had
dropped all their leaves.
apparently they had preserved their buds,
and now skeletons of bare branches where tipped with new
leaves.
here and there trees rooted in the thinnest soil remained bare,
their empty branches revealing trees that would not recover.

eventually the blue hills began to turn green as colors began to
show in the growing light.
then we could see the pastures, brown and dead only two weeks
ago, now lush with tender new grass.

along the road the johnson grass was two and three feet deep.
as is his ritual, big left the road and began walking thru the tall
grass as the time for his morning poop neared.
at first only his head and back were visible,
cutting thru the tall grass like a ship thru the waves.
when he reached the taller grass,
he was like the hidden predator in a horror movie;
nothing revealing his passage but the waving of the grass.
then he stopped and his head popped up as he squatted to attend
to business.
after a minute his head disappeared again,
and clots of dirt and grass began flying up into the air as he
kicked up his customary roostertail.
i had to laugh at the sight.
then big himself popped out of the grass,
as he returned to the road with a single bound.

as we continued our walk, i noticed a cloud glowing white in the morning sunshine.
we remained in the twilight, but;
"it won't be long now, mr big!"

it wasn't long at all.
the words had barely left my mouth before i saw the light hit the top of the tallest hill.
as big and i continued to walk, we watched the sunrise moving down the slope with remarkable speed.
the line separating night and day seemed to flow down the hillsides,
coalescing into a single line when it reached the junctions between the hills.

as we climbed to meet the sunrise, it raced to meet us.
i could see the bright blue chicory flowers starting to open in anticipation of its arrival.
as we neared the top, the light began to illuminate the tops of the trees around us.
ever the competitor, i told big we needed to hurry,
and just as the sunlight was almost to touch my head we passed around a corner,
and into the shadow of another hill.

we were safely in the shade from that point to the turnaround and back.
we were on the protected stretch of road where the snow never melts, and the sun would not reach down into its hidden reaches until nearly noon.
in the middle of winter the sun never shines there

when we came back around the corner, the sun was already high in the sky.
the chicory was blazing blue.
white fleabane stood out against the green grass like a sprinkling of powdered sugar.
thick stands of black-eyed susans painted the roadside gaily with brown and yellow.
dense patches of delicate blue and yellow asiatic dayflowers had appeared from nowhere.

as a matter of fact, the grassy predawn roadsides had been replaced with a garden rich in wildflowers.
the big white morning glories that we had admired on the way out were closing up.
but looking closer revealed a riot of flowers:
some of the blackeyed susans and fleabane were revealed as lanceleaf and daisies on closer examination.
blood red trumpet creeper abounded along the edge of the forest and the dark, rich purples of ironweed peeked out from the tall grass.
horse nettles, joe pye weed, vervain, baneberry, and vinca.
identifying my wildflowers had revealed that most are considered weeds.
it seems right that we are all here together; we rejects of society.

the worker discarded by the economy as too old, with lots of tread left.
the dog condemned as vicious by society, with a relentlessly gentle, loving temperament.
and plants denounced as weeds, with flowers of rare and special beauty.

no wonder we enjoy the special treat of watching the sun rise behind us.

i noticed that big and i had come to a stop,
looking out across the beautiful valley in front of us...
probably spared from development only because its rocky soil was too thin to perk.
big was looking up at me, wearing his wise expression in place of his usual grin.
"you're right big guy. sometimes we are so busy seeing what is wrong, that we don't see how much is right."

then we walked on;
into another perfect day, in a perfect place.

laz

08-03-12
big days that make it happen

i wasn't feeling all that hot last night.
even went to bed just past midnight
(no civilized person ever goes to bed the same day he gets up-
richard harding davis)

didn't wake up until the clock read 5:01, so i knew all was not
well.
but then, my whole body was telling me the same thing.
my head felt like it was encased in a fog
and my belly was bubbling like a witches cauldron.

my legs felt like sacks of sand as i crawled out of bed and looked
out the window.
"dadgummit"
it wasn't raining.
that reduced me to one choice. coach big would be waiting.

stepping outside did not improve my attitude a bit.
it was like someone had been waiting outside the door to wrap
me in a hot, wet, wool blanket.
big was, naturally, jumping around and wooo wooo woooing his
delight.
because big never has a bad day.
even when he was "sick as a dog" from eating that skunk,
he was still ready to go every day.
sometimes i wish i was a big.

"you're gonna have to be patient this morning, mr big. i'm not
going to be going very fast."
we went slowly down the driveway in the dark,
big being very careful not to pull.
(i have to remind myself once again, dogs don't speak english.
responding to my request is pure coincidence)

there must be a pretty heavy cloud cover,
because we are just past the full moon.
i know right where it should be,
and there is no sign of light there.
maybe it will rain and send us home early.

meanwhile, the air is so humid that i feel like i am pushing
through it.
there is not a moth wing-beat of a breeze.
yesterday's heat had not been able to escape
and i am soon sticky and sweaty.
meanwhile my gurgling stomach periodically erupts with a
sulphurous belch.
each time i can feel a gorge rise in my throat,
and wait to see if i will upchuck whatever is down there.

maybe it was something i ate?
i think back on last night's supper;
6 eggs, runny side up...
a pound of pork sausage...
a big block of cheddar cheese...
6 slices of bread with butter...
a quart of whole milk...

no, nothing there to upset my stomach. pretty much an average
supper.
maybe it was because i didn't have any habaneros to put in it?

as the ambient light grows, this is not a day for sightseeing.
mostly i look down at my feet and focus on moving them.
as rotten as i feel, i am maintaining pretty much my normal pace.
i look over at big.
he also seems to be focused on the task at hand.
the humidity is so high i think i see a bow wave peeling back off
his nose.

the clock says we hit the turn in almost exactly our normal one
hour.
of course, i am not usually having to concentrate to keep from
dragging my feet and stumbling.
i've perked up a little,
but my head is still fuzzy, and the rumbles from deep in my gut
are subsiding slowly.
my belly feels inflated...
(no need for anyone to mention that it always *looks* inflated)

halfway back i start to feel really thirsty.
that is odd, i can stack rocks in the hot sun for longer than this
before i need a drink.

thinking about that i look up to see the cloud cover is still there.
thank god.
it is miserable enough already.
the hot sun beating down would be all i needed.

i return to looking at my feet.
i see a rabbit leg coming up.
no sign of the rest of the rabbit.
just a single leg, lying in the middle of the road.
as it gets closer, i can see that it is well flattened and thoroughly
sunbaked.

big never turns down an offering from the stomach fairy.
as he comes parallel, he deftly reaches out with his paw and flips
it over in reach.
then scoops it up with his dumpster-sized mouth,
and with a couple of crunches the rabbit leg is gone.

dogs have no word for "nasty."
they have over a hundred words for crinkle
(watch them come running if you so much as touch a food
package)
but they have no word for "nasty."

big should be the one with a bubbling belly.
but he looks fairly well pleased with himself.

noticing that i am having to work to keep pace going downhill,
i don't look forward to the last climbs in that final mile.
normally they don't amount to enough to notice.
but if i am working to go downhill...

that is, if they ever get here.
i check my watch,
put my head down and try to just go for a while.
finally i check my watch again.
it has been two minutes.

and that is the way we make it home...
except for one stop as we pass jeff's house.
jeff is working in his garden,
and comes out to pet big
(along with giving me a bag of cayenne peppers he grew)

i've never been gladder to reach the driveway.
i can let big go,
he will walk right beside me all the way to the house.
once there i flop down in my yard chair and give big his
breakfast.

"thanks coach big. i'd have never got through that one without
you."

i have my eyes on another hundred miler,
and it isn't the easy days that will get me there.
days like this,
days when it isn't all fun and games,
these are the big days that will make it happen.

laz

08-15-12
the big attachment

i was sitting at my computer working,
when something made me look up.

what did i see, but the big dog coming up the steps onto the
porch, a most serious look on his face.

for the 1,000th time, he had taken off his cable.
he had a mission.

My stocky red friend came across the porch, and started at the
far end, walking up to the windows and looking inside.
after looking around inside at each one, he moved on to the next.
when he reached the last window and saw me sitting at the
computer, his broad face lit up and he wagged his tail happily.
then he lay himself down on the porch under that window.

i sat there looking at my stocky friend.
he looked so content.
i knew i couldn't leave him out there but so long.
it really is something of a quandary.
he just lets himself off because he wants to be with me
(or at least close)
and at this point, i do not believe he would go anywhere.

but he is a big. his whole life is a last chance.
a chance i can't afford to take.
after a few minutes i went out to join him.

i sat in my chair on the porch and big came over wagging his tail
happily. he walked past, stopped with his back end in front of me,
and looked at me over his shoulder.
"i shouldn't have ever introduced you to the butt scratch mr big."

he just waited expectantly.
he has a sweet spot just above the base of his tail, and i started
scratching it vigorously.
his eyes closed in ecstasy and his tongue popped in and out of his
mouth.

it only took a few moments before his knees started to buckle.
i think big loves a butt scratch even more than a belly rub.
i finally patted him on the backside, signaling an end to his butt
scratch.

"come on big guy, i'd rather pat the other end."
he sat down between my feet, leaned back, and cocked his head
to one side.
big is soooo hard to figure out.

he let out a sigh as i started scratching behind his ear.
we sat out there for a while,
big's lean turning into more of a melt,
as he sought to make as much contact with me as possible,
and we worked our way thru his numerous petting favorites.

finally i told him;
"well, big guy, you know i have stuff to do. we can't just sit out
here all day."
he got up and walked over to the steps and stopped to wait on
me to tell him to go on down.
we walked out together, big leading the way to where his cable
lay waiting.
he waited patiently while i hooked him back up,
and then leaned his huge head against my leg for a brief moment
before trotting off to the bigloo.

he went inside and turned to lie with his head in the doorway,
looking at me.
"you have a good nap, big fella, and i'll come get you for supper in
just a little while."
his eyes closed and i headed back into the house.

i wonder if any of us are really worthy of the kind of love our
dogs give us.

laz

08-20-12
bigfoot

no matter how hard we try to figure out what is going on,
the hills and woods of short creek still hold many mysteries for
me & big.

some mysteries me & big can only speculate.
we are familiar with the short creek crows.
we can keep count of the size of the murder,
as it fluctuates from year to year.
we can pretty well figure out the boundaries of their territory,
which are also subject to fluctuation.
We can generally pin down where they nest,
and when the young take to the air,
how many they successfully raised.
we have even been witness to a few crow wars,
when the short creek crows were forced to defend their territory
from neighboring murders.

this fall we saw something entirely new,
as a mega-murder of some 50-60 crows roosted down by ben's
creek for a couple of weeks. we knew that large flocks sometimes
formed around major food sources (like a dump),
but there was no food source to feed that many crows.
indeed, each morning the flock would scatter soon after sunrise,
smaller groups flying off in various directions.
each evening they reconvened to spend the night in a couple of
large trees down by ben's creek.

where this army of crows came from we never knew.
our local crows were nowhere to be found while they were here.
after a couple of weeks of their raucous calls ringing up and
down our little valley all day long,
one morning they were simply gone.
we had no more idea where they went,
than we did where they came from.
but the first day after they left,
the crows of our local murder were back in business as if nothing
had happened.
mysterious.

the stomach fairy mystery continues to be unsolved.
one day last week we found two stomachs on the same day.
big considered that a banner day.

listers scoffed at the idea that it was screech owls.
just because "screech owls swallow their food whole."
no one gave any credence to my theory that mice feeding on
genetically modified wheat had caused mutant screech owls to
develop.
screech owls that cut out the stomachs of their prey,
and dropped them on the road for pit bulls to find.

even i have to admit that the feline theory made more sense.
we do have lots of bobcats,
cats do eviscerate their prey.
and maybe bobcats don't care for stomachs.
i know that large intestines are left with about the same
frequency (and it is easy to see why a full rabbit large intestine
would be rejected as food).
i still look at it as a mystery.
i think big figures as long as tasty stomach treats keep appearing
on the road,
only a fool would ask questions.
better to believe in a stomach fairy.

remembering what happened when i decided to catch the tooth
fairy, i have to admit big's approach makes sense.

sometimes big, with his own set of finely tuned senses, knows
the answers; but i do not.
for example, the persimmon seed poops.

we have persimmon trees in abundance on the big farm.
as a matter of fact, the whole short creek area seems to be
persimmon central.
persimmons don't ripen until it frosts,
but that doesn't deter a lot of persimmon eaters...
by mid-august persimmon seeds are showing up in all kinds of
scat.

it is at about this time that the mystery poops appear.
me & big can recognize the source of most of the droppings we
see on the road.

actually i am certain that big, with his super nose, is fully aware of the source of all the poops.
including these fall-time human-sized anomalies that are packed with persimmon seeds.
big is something of a poop aficionado,
inspecting each new poop with the utmost seriousness...

city people have asked me before;
"why do so many animals poop on the road?"
now that mystery is easy to figure out.
all you have to do is go try to squat in the briers and it all becomes clear.

at any rate, i have asked big in the past;
"what in the world made that thing?"
big just looks at me and doesn't say anything.
sometimes you seem smarter when you don't say anything.
I figure he doesn't want me to laugh at him when he tells me it is bigfoot.

when you run by yourself, especially in the dark,
you might get the idea that you are in the woods all by yourself.
running or walking with a dog dispels that notion.
with their acute powers of smell and hearing,
they are aware of the animals hiding in the woods and watching you go by.

if i am with little or sophie, they alert me to the unseen observers by growling and raising their hackles.
like big, i have come to realize that little and sophie are easily panicked.
when they start barking during the day i follow big's lead.
he generally just looks at them like they are idiots.
if big barks too, there is really something there.
so i don't worry about what little and sophie tell me.
when big alerts me i am worried.
the only familiar thing big fears are bicycles.
and i know there are no bicyclists watching us from the woods in the dark.

all the usual animals, big has learned that he can't chase.
rabbits and squirrels, deer and cows.
even turkeys and buzzards, big just looks at them as we pass.

he does raise his hackles at skunks.
ever since the stink-cat episode he harbors a particular grudge
towards skunks.
but i know when it is a skunk hiding in the darkness.
that doesn't require the sensitive sniffer of a big.

every once in a long while,
we pass something mysterious in the woods.
big's hair stands on end, in a strip two inches wide,
all the way down his back.
he looks back and forth into the woods,
trying to spot that something as we walk past.
i have asked him what it is, but he doesn't answer.
he looks up at me briefly,
and then goes back to scanning the woods.
i figure it has to be bigfoot...
come to see if the persimmons are ripe yet.

but big doesn't have all the advantages.
his life has its own mysteries, and sometimes i know the answer.
for example, the tragic disappearance of amy.
i know where she was all summer (cape cod)
and big only knows she was gone.

he has never trusted sophie to look after amy.
he has always barked a warning when amy goes out with sophie
on the leash.
his worst fears were realized at the start of the summer.
sophie went off with amy one day, and they didn't come back.
it was a couple of weeks before sophie showed back up...

and amy wasn't with her.

as the weeks turned into months,
big finally gave up looking for amy.
big knows that people sometimes leave, and never come back.
it has happened to him too many times.
he probably thought that bigfoot got her.

this time he was lucky.
about the time we started finding the bigfoot poops,
packed with persimmon seeds,
amy showed back up one day.

you have never seen such a happy dog.
amy is his special charge.

big life is back to normal.
amy has even taken him on a few runs.
his only worry is that she seemed to have learned nothing.
she still goes out running with the unreliable sophster.

this morning big & i had barely returned from doing the goat
corner loop when amy and sophie came out the door.
big was elated to see amy.
i had just gotten his breakfast out,
but he was more than willing to postpone it and go running with
amy.
when amy and sophie went down the steps, big ran over to the
top of the steps and looked at me for permission to go with them.
"no, big guy. you need to stay here. maybe amy will take you for a
run when she gets back."
he was visibly disappointed, but big does what he is told.

i got to see what big does when amy and sophie go running.
he watches for her.
not "waits" for her,
meaning listening for the sounds of her return.
he watches for her.
actively, continuously, with intensity.
he ran over and stood at the very edge of the porch and watched
them disappear, his ears cocked.
he held that position long after she had gone out of sight.
finally he ran over to the other end of the porch and assumed the
same position, looking down into the woods
he was looking in the direction where the road passes by the
bottom of our hill.
it was a safe bet that amy was passing that spot.
(normally he barks at her when she reaches that point, but he
was on the porch and we don't bark on the porch)

after amy & sophie got out of earshot,
big returned to his post looking down the driveway.
after a while he lay down and propped his chin on one of my big
fossil rocks,
so he could keep looking down the drive.

his ears were pricked up, and he stared with laser intensity.
he might have been reclined, but he was not relaxed.
sophie has lost amy before. she is not reliable.
and it is persimmon season...bigfoot is here.
(we have seen his poops)

big eventually decided he ought to eat his breakfast.
he came and stood by his bowl, staring down the driveway and
pricking his ears in case there was the faintest sound.
finally he grabbed a mouthful of food, chewed and swallowed,
then ran back to the edge of the porch to look and listen twice as
hard.
he might have missed something while all he could hear was his
food crunching...
and amy is his personal responsibility.
once he was certain he had missed nothing he returned to his
food bowl and stood by it, staring down the driveway and
pricking his ears in case there was the faintest sound.
finally he grabbed a mouthful of food, chewed and swallowed,
then ran back to the edge of the porch to look and listen twice as
hard. he might have missed something while all he could hear
was his food crunching...

and that was how big ate his breakfast.
one bite at a time.

after eating, he came over for some cuddling and petting.
but we had to be lined up where he could see down the driveway
at all times...

and we had to stop every time he thought he heard a sound,
so he could run over and make sure it wasn't amy.

periodically he would study the woods in the direction of where
the road passes the bottom of the hill.
amy comes back that way sometimes.

finally we heard the dogs at the pug house barking
and big lit up.
that had to mean amy was coming home.
we were told that lynnor's pug is dead,
that he had been bitten by a rattlesnake.
i considered that proof snakes are not allied with the devil.

if they were the pug would never have been bitten
(professional courtesy)
but amy saw him friday...

at any rate, she didn't see him today,
but there are plenty of nuisance dogs left at the pug house
(with or without the pug)
to let big know his amy is almost home.
big ran to the edge of the porch and looked down the driveway
with his tail wagging
for about 10 more minutes until amy finally came into sight.
i relented and gave him permission to go greet her.

big's ordeal was behind him until amy goes out tomorrow
morning,
putting her life on the line with only sophie to protect her...

it is a risk any time.
but right now it is especially dangerous.
bigfoot is in the neighborhood for the persimmon harvest.

laz

09-01-12
twas the night before hell

me and big had done a lot of miles together since he rescued me.
during all those miles, something in his indomitable spirit had
inspired me.
once i had been an ultramarathon runner,
able to cover hundreds of miles.
when big found me,
it seemed like those days were all behind me.

but big never gave up.
no matter what happened, he remained positive.
big simply never considered that things might not work out,
and when he wanted something,
he went after it.
nothing ever stood in big's way.

100 miles is a magical distance for ultrarunners,
and something in me wanted to reach that magical distance one
more time.
with coaches big and little training me,
something in me came to believe that it was possible.
once the idea took root,
everything else just seemed to fall into place.

there was the perfect race.
the bloody 11-W hundred had a soft enough time limit
that i had a chance to finish.
my old friend, durb (steve durbin) wanted to run it with me for
old times sake
(we had done a lot of miles together over the years)
another friend, terri preast, was willing to crew for us.

i hated to leave my big behind,
but somehow, i thought he would understand.
there was a dream to chase, just one more time.

and so it was that september the first found me in Knoxville,
fitfully trying to get to some sleep.
for, in the morning, i would be facing the supreme test.

the pre-race dinner was a success.
the pre-race sleep did not come so easy.
my mind went over and over what was coming...

clothes are laid out, and mere hours to go before we toe the line...
or is that toe the curb?

terri the angel was here for dinner.
i don't have juli's gift for telling how good people are,
but the people who have made this possible deserve her kind of
praise.

the combination of anticipation and fear tastes so sweet....
like chocolate and hot peppers (and i even have some of that!)
in just a few hours it starts to get real.

at the pre-race meal there were some folks talking really small.
they seriously think they are going to make a run at dead last.
just wait till they see me in action.

laz (one of the dirty dozen)

09-06-12
not this day

i don't think i ever doubted that i would finish.

i had some well-founded fears about what it might take,
but i knew i would finish.
what choice did i have?

i haven't ever been a big enthusiast about "dedicated" races.
i can't see myself ever running a race for someone else.
ultimately we, or at least i, have to do the races for ourselves.
the responsibility of a relay is something different altogether.
you might run the race for yourself,
but in a relay,
if you quit, you quit on everybody.

i couldn't quit on naresh.
naresh is a young guy,
he didn't have to spend his time and resources to organize a race
with a time limit within the reach of the old guys.
i couldn't quit on durb.
durb is a lot faster than me.
he probably made his race twice as hard
(and surely twice as long)
by running with me so we could share resources.
i couldn't quit on terri.
she could have spent labor day weekend doing something fun.
maybe even something that allowed time for sleep!
terri was the kind of crew you dream about.
she understood the crew job exactly.
the crew is not to provide comfort or ease suffering.
the crew is there to allow you to stop as little as possible.
and most of all i couldn't quit on the guys who deserved to be
there.
i heard from a lot of them.
people more deserving of this one last chance than me;
encouraging me, rooting for me.

talking about it prior to the race,
i found there was general agreement on the advantages the old

guys bring to races.
there is experience,
and...

well, experience and not much else.
i had a little bit else.
i had my responsibility to the team.

we left knoxville in the light of a full moon,
walking steadily.
i had on my favorite shoes, soft and well-worn.
they felt really good on my feet, but i knew they wouldn't last the
whole race.
the forefoot was worn so thin i could step on a dime, and read
the date.
that wouldn't matter for a while.
But eventually it would matter a lot.

i focused on enjoying the scenery and counting the miles.
i always hate the part of the race where it doesn't seem like you
have gotten anywhere.
until the first 30 miles are in the bank it doesn't seem real.
these days those first 30 miles take a long time.

we had to settle for reaching intermediate goals,
like seeing the start of clinch mt when we reached blaine.
at 140 miles long, it reaches well into virginia.
we would be alongside it's base for about the next 70 miles,
before turning to the east.

with us hitting 2.5 miles an hour like clockwork,
and terri performing like a pro,
so that we could never stop moving,
the 12 hour goal for 30 miles was met exactly.
a couple of hours later it finally came time for a break,
and i switched to my second (and best quality) pair of shoes.

for those who don't know it,
11-w has a lot more history than just its tenure as one of the
nation's most dangerous roads.
as the natural route thru one of the oldest geologic features in
north america,
it follows the route of the lee highway,

one of the first stagecoach roads into tennessee,
the main indian trail down the holston valley,
and the migratory trails of millions of years of animals back to
the days of the dinosaurs.
durb was kept busy snapping pictures of 200 year old houses
and various other relics.

the day was hotter than we had hoped it would be,
a whole lot more humid.
and the town of rutledge seemed to take forever arriving.
we amused ourselves by spotting a firetower atop clinch
mountain, and talking about how many there used to be up there.
an hour later durb commented; "there's another firetower."
it was the same one.
distant landmarks don't give much satisfaction when you move
fast. at our pace objects atop clinch mt seemed to stay in view for
half a day.

good fortune held as we finally came to rutledge proper,
and arrived at the local hardees just as i was ready for a major pit
stop.
indoor plumbing is man's greatest invention, after fire.
when we went inside we found paul, frank, and TJ were already
there rehydrating and taking a rest stop of their own.

it was a surprise to catch anyone during a race,
even more of a surprise this early.
but terri was proving to be a powerful secret weapon.
we left the trio there, and hurried back out on the road.
the 2-lane didn't end until bean station, at 40 miles,
and we wanted to finish as much of it as possible before dark.

as we moved down the road we kept watch behind us for the trio
we'd left in rutledge.
eventually we saw tj's figure in the distance.
he'd make up ground running, and then fall back walking.
knowing how slow i am, tj will have to improve his walking
technique in the future.

i had thought of the 11-w course as a perfect course,
lots of mountain views, but no major hills.
running it we discovered there were more than plenty of climbs
and descents.

atop one climb i spotted the familiar shape of short mountain in the distance.
amidst all the granite and limestone hills,
it was an anomalous mountain of sand.
a silica company mining operation has left huge scars that can be seen from great distances.
atop the mountain was a tall tower,
whose blinking red lights we would chase all night long.

after a few hours terri suggested toasted cheese sandwiches.
durb & i were game.
we'd been moving almost nonstop for about 15 hours and were starting to feel a little wear.
with 2/3 of the race ahead of us we didn't need to kill ourselves just yet.
terri located a perfect spot for a picnic,
the parking lot of a factory in tate springs.
she even found a table in the trash pile next to the dumpsters.
tj caught up soon after we stopped, and joined us for supper.

it was sort of like a family cookout as terri whipped out rich delicious toasted cheese sandwiches on a camp stove,
and we greedily scarfed them down.
it was here we dubbed our little excursion the "roving camping trip in hell."

we left tj still sitting in the parking lot as we headed out into the darkness.
just a few more miles and we would reach bean station and wide shouldered 4-lane.

as we trudged thru the darkness word trickled back about the action up ahead.
naresh and some others were having blister problems.
there had been some drops.
at least one unfortunate runner had missed the turn at bean station, and ran all the way to clinch mountain on the wrong road. experience was moving us up in the field.
my feet (altho slowly growing sore from the hours of unbroken walking) were unscathed by blisters.
i had studied the route carefully and committed all the turns to memory.

it was almost midnight by the time we came out of bean station. short mountain, apparently looming over us, was still an hour or more away.
midnight to sunup is prime time for the open road runner.
traffic fades to nothing, and the runner has the road to himself.
i moved out into the traffic lanes to find a more comfortable track.

as we followed the highway's huge loop around short mountain i encountered another problem.
some of the uphill slopes were too steep for the blood supply in my bad leg,
and i had to slow down considerably to get up them.
there were going to be a lot of hills like that on the remainder of the course.

altho i was delving into distances far beyond what i had attempted since the surgery,
i still had set out certain intermediate goals.
30 miles in 12 hours we had nailed.
besting my time at 42 miles (the furthest i had gone) was achieved.
reaching the halfway point (56 miles) in 24 hours turned out to be a lot more challenging.
i found myself pushing hard down the long descent on the far side of short mountain.
by the time we reached the bottom, and the halfway point, just a little over my goal,
i found myself just about wasted, and we had to take another break.
anything i had made up in the frantic last couple of hours was gone before we got moving again
and the predawn light revealed that we would be starting up a long, steep climb.

when i stood up on my feet again, they hurt like heck.
in what would be the pattern after every stop the rest of the race i hobbled away extremely slowly as the pain in my feet slowly subsided and my stiff legs loosened up.
durb, meanwhile, would let me get way on up the road before he started. steve didn't have a problem running fast, he needed breaks to stretch his bad back.

we had worked out our routine over the first 24 hours,
me leaving steve behind and him running to catch up.
i couldn't move fast, so i couldn't afford to ever stop.
durb couldn't survive continuous motion.
terri, somehow, managed to keep us both fed and hydrated.

a couple of hours later i got the thrill of the race.
reaching the motel in rogersville (61 miles) what did i see but a
staggering figure coming out the front door.
it was naresh.
the look of surprise on his face,
to find himself run down,
was worth a million dollars.

naresh walked with me for a mile or so before he warmed to the
task and took off on his blistered feet.
durb, meanwhile had gotten much further behind than usual.
walking thru lovely rogersville, i wondered if he was going to be
able to hold out and make the whole distance.

rogersville marked the end of the part of the race with a definite
plan. i had held out a remote hope that i could finish in close to
48 hours.
that was obviously out of reach.
while i had used to be able to go for 48 hours on a single 15
minute nap,
it was obvious i wouldn't be close to that.
during the night, durb and i had cobbled out a plan:
run until it got really hot on the second day,
then get a room for a few hours of air conditioned sleep.
if we got far enough we should be able to finish the run in one
more big push.
terri concurred.

we got lucky sunday morning and had cloud cover until noon.
even tho i was still going really slow because of my foolish predawn push, we managed to get to 67 miles in a little over 30
hours before the steaming heat and humidity convinced us it was
time for a serious break.

while terri drove us back to the rogersville motel, we planned
our break like a pit stop.
when we hit the motel everyone was doing something the whole

time, and the shower stayed in constant use.
in a matter of minutes everyone was clean, fed, and in bed.

i lay down expecting sleep to be almost instantaneous.
instead i had this incredible pain come from nowhere to engulf
my bad leg.

on a scale of 1-10,
extracting my own molar without anesthetic rates about a 7.
this was a 9.

my leg was twitching uncontrollably and i had to clench my jaws
to keep from hollering.
i wished i was alone, because i would have liked to holler.
after a few minutes i started to worry that even my muffled
sounds were keeping durb and terri awake.
i listened to hear their steady deep breathing.
i needn't have worried.
after 31 continuous hours on the road they could have slept thru
a train wreck.
for the first time i started to feel some doubt.
i finally got my leg to quit jumping around like a frog leg in a
frying pan,
but the waves of excruciating pain wouldn't let up.
i wondered what i had done to my leg.
i wondered if there was any way i would be able to go on when i
woke up.
i wondered if i would even be able to sleep.
and then i joined my companions in dreamland...
my eyes popped open of their own accord.
i could still hear the steady deep breathing of terri and durb
i looked at my watch, but wasn't sure if i had slept for 4 hours or
5.
either way, it was a good night's (or in this case day's) sleep.
we hadn't discussed how long to sleep,
i was certain that i would get plenty of sleep by my standards.
durb & terri needed to get whatever they thought they needed,
i was sure that would be more than i am used to.
they were the ones making the sacrifices on my behalf,
so there was no need to kill them.
i lay there enjoying the way that nothing hurt.

i moved my bad leg tentatively,
wondering if the horrible pain would return...

nothing.
i wasn't sure how it could have recovered,
but i wasn't looking any gift horse in the mouth.

moments later terri's alarm went off and i heard the others
stirring.
the first thing steve did was open the curtains.
i was disappointed to see rain streaks running down the
windowpane.
so i immediately did what me & big learned during the months of
rain last fall, i turned on the tv and found weather radar.
it showed a narrow band of heavy rain passing right over us.
behind it was clear skies.
so we knew that if we dawdled a bit getting ready,
we could avoid wet feet that much longer.
this was the leading edge of the hurricane isaac weather,
so more rain would be coming,
but the longer we kept our feet dry,
the longer we could stay blister free.

i taped my feet and applied a little extra vaseline,
then donned my third and final pair of shoes.
they were a pretty old pair with many thousands of miles,
and sort of clunky.
but they had a metatarsal pad in them.
i don't like to put the pads in my shoes, as they are permanent
and they aren't all that comfortable.
earlier in the run, the neuroma pain had helped balance the pain
between my legs and keep me from limping.
at this point there was enough pain in my good leg without it.
plus, it was likely my shoes would get wet soon enough.
i did not want to get more than one pair wet.
so these shoes would have to finish the race.

driving back out to where we stopped,
we congratulated ourselves on our planning.
we had missed both the blistering heat and a torrential
downpour while we slept.

we saw paul and frank about a mile and a half from where we
would start.

this time we were the fresh runners.
we had kept enough track of them to know they had either not
slept at all, or had slept outside.
either way, they had faced both the heat and the rain, and would
be really tired.

terri had picked us up right before the course crossed a bridge.
we were amused to find that it crossed "big creek" and had to
stop for some more pictures.

after we got our big pictures made we started off closing in on
the turn to surgoinsville.
altho it was still a mile or two away, we could see the turn as we
ran.
it was a relief to see virtually no traffic going that way.
it would be dark soon after we got on that stretch, and it had no
real shoulders.

i was anticipating the surgoinsville section almost as much as the
rogersville stretch.
when the new 11-w was built, it cut straight thru the hills and cut
off the loop of old 11-w that goes thru surgoinsville.
the surgoinsville section gave us excellent views of the history of
our route up the holston valley.

the early settlers down the holston valley followed the main
indian trail
(named the "great indian war path" by the early settlers)
which had followed the animal migratory trails that existed
when the indians first arrived.
the unique geography of the holston valley, with virtually all hills
running in parallel lines,
created an unusually good route for land travel prior to the
building of roads.
in 1761 a man named henry timberlake was sent as a peace
envoy to the "overhill cherokee" who lived along the tennessee
river, at the request of the cherokee themselves
(who had sent a 400 man delegation/force to ask for peace.)
traveling down the holston river valley, timberlake elected to
take his own party down the river in canoes rather than to risk

an arduous overland journey.
the indians, traveling much the same route that we followed in
the race reached the end of the river first,
and had to wait for days for the river travellers to catch up.
by 1825 a stagecoach road had been built along the original
indian trails.
the standards for stagecoach roads were to have a level track 15
feet wide along the entire route,
altho the wooden bridges that crossed creeks were only 12 feet
wide.
given the limitations of animal drawn transport to climb steep
grades, the stagecoach road followed the original trails fairly
faithfully.
where steeper slopes had to be crossed, the roads were cut at an
angle up the hills.
due to the arduous nature of cutting roads with entirely muscle
power, here and there narrow passages were circumvented.
sometimes it was easier to "switchback" up, or go around a hill,
rather than to hand drill rock for extensive blasting.
for nearly 100 years the old stagecoach road served as the major
artery for traffic up and down the valley.

in the early 1920s the first cross country roadway, the lee
highway, was constructed, from washington, dc to san diego.
it followed the old stagecoach road down the holston river valley.
to make the lee highway, the road underwent another level of
improvement.
wooden bridges were replaced by twin drystone foundations,
topped by a single horizontal concrete slab.
a road-base was built to accomodate the heavier motorized
vehicles.
and it was suddenly possible to straighten climbs because of
those vehicle's greater ability to climb grades.

in addition, the advent of motor powered road construction
equipment made it feasible to cut through and remove obstacles.
as a result many small segments of the "old stagecoach road"
were bypassed, and left intact.
we saw many of those as we made our way
along the bloody 11-w.

In 1929 the road was included in a major north-south route,
us highway 11.
then came one of the most unlikely boons to rural america, the
great depression.
putting the throngs of unemployed to work building
infrastructure opened up the country to travel.
11-w was one of the beneficiaries.
while rogersville was a "major" city along the old route,
surgoinsville was just a tiny place.
coming out of surgoinsville, the lee highway had wound its way
along the bottomlands to reach rogersville.
a few miles southwest of surgoinsville, the "new" 11-w turned
west and by using existing hollows and cutting through a few
hills it took a more direct route to rogersville.
as in many places along the way, an old section of the lee
highway was left exactly as it had originally lay.
it is still in use as a local road, along with one of the original rock
and concrete bridges that we can see as we pass.
the depression era 11-w bridges were all concrete, with concrete
"guardrails."

to many of us older folks, they are a reminder of the roadways of
our childhood.
when the newest version of 11-w came along, surgoinsville was
cut off altogether.
now it remains as a small southern town along a side road,
frozen in the fifties.
the depression era 11-W is an impressive tribute to the quality of
work done during that depression infrastructure boom,
its cuts and embankments still looking almost pristine.
going thru surgoinsville, the old stagecoach road parallels the
newer highway, sticking to the more easily altered landscape.
surgoinsville is a rare treat.
all along the way we got to see sections of the predecessors of
today's roads and bridges
(except the wooden bridges, which no longer exist!)
on the surgoinsville loop it all comes together at once.

one thing we cannot say about any part of the 11-w is;
"in no time at all"
unless we are talking about those car-things that everyone seems
to have.

115

they cover a lot of ground, really fast!
On foot we covered the ground, really slow!
none the less, between the anticipation of the surgoinsville loop,
and not being near as sore as we expected
(not to mention the freshest we would be for the rest of the race)
it seemed like we reached the surgoinsville turnoff pretty quick.
getting onto a quiet 2-lane was a relief.

we had traveled only a short distance when we came to a
historical marker.
it seems that back in 1788 the settlers of the big creek were
holed up in their big fort, beseiged by indians.
the man honored on the marker had brought relief to them,
at the cost of his life.
the indians spotted him, and mortally wounded the guy,
but he managed to reach the fort and deliver the desperately
needed supplies before he died.
what was it that was so vital it was worth dying to deliver?
salt!

many an ultrarunner understands.

what also struck us as interesting was the location.
obviously he could not approach fort big along the main trail,
but instead he had to find another route to slip in by.
it was no coincidence that he chose the route that would one day
be selected for a new motor roadway...
the one now called "old" 11-w.

distractions like the surgoinsville loop make the time pass faster,
so it didn't seem like any time before we had to cross the road to
let a car pass.
then there was another...
and another...
and then more and more, coming both ways.
we had to criss-cross the road to avoid them,
and even ended up having to wade into the tall, wet grass
alongside the road a few times.
this was met with great displeasure,
as we had tried so hard to keep our feet dry.

this went on for about 20 minutes before it started to tail off,
leaving us baffled as to where all these cars had come from?

finally it dawned on us that it was sunday night...
church had just let out.

after the church traffic died down we were left to enjoy our trek
in peace.
we talked about the sights we were seeing, and the history we
could feel all around us.
once we passed surgoinsville we came to a series of really steep,
painful hills.
even in the darkness we could make out the cuts where long-ago
roadways had zig-zagged their way up the hills,
and we sort of wished that option was still available.
we reached new 11-w near midnight, and this time it was the
durb who got lucky.
a little country store was minutes away from closing.
they lacked indoor plumbing, but did have a porta-pottie.
terri (who we were now referring to as "our angel")
was cooking a nice supper of brats.
sitting down for a few minutes was a welcome relief,
but a mixed blessing.
starting back up had become quite painful.

we had only been back on the road for a few minutes when i saw
a truly funny marquee, reading:
"Dusty Bibles Leads an Evil Life"
i assumed the building behind it was a strip club.
then i noticed it was actually a church,
and the sign said;
"Dusty Bibles Lead to an Evil Life"
the brain was starting to short-circuit.

from where we returned to the highway, all the way to kingsport
in the early 90's of miles was a straight shot.
it would take forever to top each hill,
only to see the road stretching endlessly to the next hill.
we passed thru small towns without seeing a car.
the occasional passing vehicle on the highway could be heard for
10 minutes before it came in sight.
my feet and legs were starting to hurt pretty consistently,
but i was more worried about the durb.
his back was really giving him trouble.

a couple of rainbands passed thru,
but each time terri showed up quickly,
and gave us a chance to hop in the van and wait it out.
despite our prompt rescues, my feet were getting irreversibly
wet.

we took another short sitting break at some indefinite distance,
and when we started back i hobbled pathetically before numbing
back into effective movement.
the tradeoff between a desperate need to take a break,
and the horror of starting back,
was getting to be a difficult choice.
the only bright spot was that we were right on pace to finish part
2 in 24 hours.
we weren't going fast, but we weren't slowing down.
steve had to be back at work on tuesday,
and could not afford to finish as late as i would.
so we had agreed to separate when we reached kingsport.
terri was confident that she could still crew us both.
those car-things are so fast it is amazing.

shortly before morning twilight we finally reached the holston
crossing, marking our entry into kingsport.
morning traffic was getting heavier by the minute,
and visibility was poor.
the bridge over the holston had no shoulder, just 4 traffic lanes,
but i knew that it had a pedestrian walkway on one side.

now, why would you build a bridge with a pedestrian walkway,
and then put the guardrail across the entrance to the walkway?
i still have not any guess to the logic there,
but if it was for the purpose of watching a couple of beat-up old
men struggle to climb over, it was a success.
at both ends.
once past the holston, we took one last break together.

as we had been doing, i started first and walked so far without
seeing him that i began to wonder if steve had given it up.
he finally caught up and instead of passing walked with me for a
short distance.
when terri came by, the durb stopped again.
i was over halfway across kingsport before i saw him again.

this time he went past me with only a brief greeting.
the next time i saw him he would be finished.

it didn't take long to appreciate how important durb had been.
worrying about his back was the best thing that i had going.
now i had time to think about what faced me.
i had been under the impression that crossing the holston was 5
miles short of the 100.
but i didn't have anything really solid to base that on.
i wanted it to be 95, but believed that might only be a product of
wishful thinking.
so when terri passed i asked her to measure out to the 100 mile
mark and then back.
then i walked as hard as i could go, trying to reduce the distance
as much as i could before she returned.

i was also motivated now by the thoughts of frankenlilly.
since leaving frank and paul behind on the road to surgoinsville
we had gotten sporadic reports in their location.
there was a consistent report that paul had, or was going to drop.
some one called them frank and lilly instead of frank and paul.
in my addled state i heard that as frankenlilly, and found it
hilariously funny.
i had held my arms out in front of me and walked stiff-legged
going "URRR, URRR, URRR!"
durb laughed like it was a riot,
terri looked at us like we were slightly unbalanced.
but then, terri had gotten to grab a few cat-naps.
if you want to go into standup comedy, seek out audiences that
are hallucinating from lack of sleep.

i thought back on the reports during the night.
at one point he was said to be 6 miles behind us.
at another, someone said 2.
and that was the most recent report.
if it was correct, he was bearing down on me like a freight train
(holding his arms out straight, walking stiff-legged, and going
"URRRR, URRRR, URRR")
durb had already left me in his dust,
it seemed totally unfair that frankenlilly might knock me back
another spot so close to the finish.
i tried to tell myself that he couldn't be feeling all that great,

and i was still moving steadily, hardly ever stopping.
then i remembered that he looked like a pretty tough guy.
unfortunately, i am not very tough at all.

terri returned and told me that she couldn't find the 100 mile
mark, but i was 5 1/2 miles from the city limits.
(oh crap, the 100 mile mark is a mile and a half past that!)
i was not happy at all, but tried to keep that to myself.

i walked on, trying to go even faster,
while terri went ahead to check on steve.

i walked and walked,
then i saw abi running down the road.
she joined me and i immediately asked the number one question;
"how far am i from 100 miles?"
"oh, about 5 miles."
that was depressing news.
every time i asked, i was still 5 miles away.
as if in response to my mood, it started to rain again.
i opened the huge umbrella i had been carrying and held it over
my head in a futile gesture.
my feet were already wet,
and the darn thing was wrenched back and forth by the
backdraft off passing vehicles,
which also sprayed me with water.
i didn't really care.

the course had been climbing since i crossed the holston,
and as i left kingsport the climb kept getting steeper and steeper.
i never realized what a nasty stretch of road this was.
all i could do was walk as hard as i could go, and try to get some
of that last 5 miles out of the way.

about a lifetime later, terri came back.
she seemed so proud of herself.
"i found the 100 mile mark!"
i only wanted to know one thing;
"how far is it?"
she proudly told me;
"five miles!"

"FIVE MILES!"
i was like a petulant child.
"five miles? it is always 5 miles. i walk my butt off, and it is still 5
miles. it was 5 miles before and it is still 5 miles. i am never going
to finish if you don't let it get past 5 miles."
"would you like to sit down a few minutes?"
"i might as well. i'll get to the finish just as fast. and my feet hurt."

after a few minutes i started to feel more like myself.
this time, i reasoned, it was really 5 miles.
the other measurements had all been wrong.
if i walked again, it was going to be less.
i prayed i was right, and that i had not died and gone to hell.

i asked her when the rain would ever end.
"soon. i looked on radar and it is only raining in spots."
"well, that spot must be following me. it's been raining forever."
i left still carrying that silly and useless umbrella.

within 100 yards the rain stopped.
100 yards later i wanted it back.
the sun came out and things started heating up fast.
i sucked it up and pushed as hard as i could go.

this time the distance started to diminish.
not half as fast as seemed fair,
but at least i was less than 5 miles from the finish.

when i finally (and i mean FINALLY!) arrived at the 100 mile
mark there was a crowd.
naresh and sal were there. abi was there. terri was there.
all the frustration melted away.
i lit a cigarette to celebrate and looked up ahead.
the road, which had been climbing since the holston, turned
steeper than any time since the race started.
i just shrugged to myself and started to trudge up the hill.
i had told naresh when he was distributing race information to
be sure and emphasize that runners could stop at 100 and still
get credit for finishing the fun run.
i was counting that as an advantage for me.
facing 12 more miles after 100, especially when 100 counts as a
finish.
that is mentally difficult.

i had been counting on passing some folks at that point since i
signed up for the race.

while i was plugging away up the hill, everyone else scattered.
i finally topped that hill, only to find an even steeper downhill,
followed by yet another killer climb.
the sun had returned and was making up for lost time,
beating down on me cruelly.
as i kept going up and down steep hills, the sun just kept getting
hotter, and i kept pushing as hard as i could go.

i thought back to the talk after i reached the 100 mile mark.
terri was going to go crew steve thru the finish, then she was
taking him back to knoxville to pick up his car.
naresh was going to crew me after terri left,
but first he and sal were going to knoxville to pick up a car.
abi had offered to help me out,
but she was off checking on other runners.
for all i knew she might be headed home after that.
it suddenly dawned on me that everyone might believe that
someone else was crewing for me.

i took stock of my situation.
i had no water.
no food.
no money.
no ID.
no phone.
i had been pushing really hard in high heat and humidity,
on a nasty hilly course.
there was not a lick of shade,
and there weren't any houses near the road.
while i had stopped hallucinating after the sun came up,
my mind was fried
(enough so that i let everyone leave without knowing if anyone
would come back)
and i still had a good 6 hours before i could finish.
i decided it was time to slow down...

 a lot.

eventually i was thrilled beyond belief to see a white van pull off
the road in front of me.

it was terri!!!
(and i thought she looked like an angel before)
by the time she arrived i was reduced to staggering down the
road, weaving like a drunk.
i had been surprised when a cop car passed me earlier without
stopping to question me.

terri looked very concerned.
she had to go back, durb was about to finish.
but she didn't want to leave me here looking like death
(and barely coherent)
i convinced her that all i needed was to cool down a little.
i wasn't that bad off, just way overheated.
i asked for 5 minutes in the front seat with the AC on my head.
as soon as i sat down, i went to sleep.
terri gave me 15 minutes.
i woke up feeling like a new man.
terri was hesitant at first, still wanting to take me with her,
but i was pretty convincing,
and very determined not to do anything that would make this
nightmare last longer.

terri came and checked on me one last time with the durb in tow.
i had 8 miles left and felt pretty good (all things considered)
so she left me with a water bottle and the pair headed for
knoxville.
it was kind of sad, after all she had done, that she wouldn't be
there for the finish.
but i simply wasn't fast enough.

at the pace i was moving,
8 miles meant another 4 hours on the road.
i think we all hate this part of the race.
knowing you can make it,
but still facing hours of effort before we can finally stop.
i just tried not to think about it and let the time pass without
notice.

every time i reached the end of a long stretch,
i sneaked a look back.
the closer i got to the finish,
the less i felt frankenlilly was going to appear.

and there wouldn't be anything i could do about it if he came
running past.
i was going as fast as i could go.

at this point in the course,
the miles matched up exactly with the mile markers,
so each one was like a separate victory.
i just couldn't understand how these mile markers were so much
farther apart than the ones back in knoxville.
naresh should really reverse the direction of the course,
so we could run those short miles at the end instead of the
beginning.

as i got nearer and nearer to bristol,
i saw dark clouds forming ahead of me.
by the time i crossed the interstate, with 3 miles to go,
i could see flashes of lightning.
a few minutes later the first few drops splattered around me.
soon i was getting pelted by a freezing cold rain.
bloody 11-w was not letting me off without the most discomfort
it could deliver.

the final mile in tennessee took almost forever,
but when i arrived at the virginia state line, with one mile to go,
total,
i took one last look behind me.
no frankenlilly. no foot-traffic at all.
i was safe in place. i would finish 5th out of 11 starters.
not so long ago running a 100 at all was an unlikely dream.
i never in my most optimistic moments imagined a top half
finish.

i could see 11-e a long time before i finally got there.
step by step i finished off my real opponent; 11-w.
there was a small cluster of people waiting for me at the finish;
sandra had come to surprise me.
chrys was there, and kyle.
naresh and abi.
everyone looked to be as happy for me as i was for myself.
there was a sense of exultation over the final few steps.
don't tell me what i can't do, the silent message went out.
don't ever tell me what i can't do.

i thought how it would feel to tell the various doctors who had
written me off what i had done.
the experts who had told me i would never run again,
or even walk.
since that day, i have taken each day as a new challenge.
a new battle to hold on to what brings me joy;
the freedom of the open road.
i took the last step on 11-w; the next step would be on 11-e,
so i raised my bad leg high and stomped my foot down in victory.
pain shot from my foot all the way to my hip,
i stumbled and nearly went down.
then i caught myself and went to celebrate with my friends.

i know one day time will win. and the experts will be right.
but not this day.

laz

09-08-12
i knew you'd come

the number one question about my bloody 11-w effort had
nothing to do with the run.
no one was interested in my hydration, or electrolytes, or food,
or even my shoes.
the number one subject of interest was big,
and would he make me do 5 miles the day after the race.

well, he didn't get the chance.
my bad leg didn't need to go straight from a 112 mile run
to 5 or 6 hours in a car,
so i didn't go home until the next morning.
big was overjoyed to see me when i did get home,
but he isn't that anxious to go for a walk after the temperature
gets up in the 90's.
instead we spent the afternoon on the porch, just hanging out.
making up for lost time.

when our first walk turned out to be not only incredibly slow,
but extremely short
(like, to the mailbox and back... with rest stops)
big didn't act at all disappointed.
i took my time walking back up the hill,
so the big fella had a chance to do some running around in the
woods.
we would walk together until he saw something interesting,
then he'd look up at me asking permission.
"go ahead big guy, check it out."
off big would go, tongue flapping in the wind,
to run a squirrel up a tree, or just to bound around loving life in
the woods.
he never went very far, and in a few minutes he'd be back;
wagging his tail, taking up his position at my side, and looking up
at me.
big is pretty serious about his job.
and his job is to walk with me.

that night amy & i were watching a football game.
talking, ironically enough, about how we wished we were as

good as our dogs think we are.
big's unwavering belief in me sets a standard that is hard to live
up to.

sophie had been pestering amy for a while,
and amy finally figured out that she needed to go outside for a
minute.
i was thinking how i was lucky,
big can almost talk and it is easy to know what he needs.
when amy came back in she remarked;
"it's raining out there."
then she added;
"and big is barking."

i reached for my boots immediately.
big doesn't bark for nothing.
"did you check on him?"
i saw amy reach for her shoes.
"i didn't have a light."
i did a quick lace-up on my boots and went to get my headlamps.
(they were still packed from the 11-w race)
"was it his 'help me' bark?"
"i don't know his barks like you do. it sounded like his 'come pet
me' bark to me."
i gave amy the dim headlight and put the good one on myself.
(such a good parent)
we went out the back door and sure enough it was pouring rain...
and big was barking.
"that is his 'help me' bark."
"i don't know his barks like you do... i'm sorry big, we're coming."
i could hear the regret in amy's voice and i felt guilty.
i shouldn't always be so blunt. i was the one who should have
heard the rain and checked on big.

as we rounded the corner i shined my light at the bigloo.
i was hoping to see his eyes shining there.
he would call for help if it was just his tarp down.
no such luck.
then i saw his eyes shining in the edge of the woods.
that was odd. i knew of no obstacle there that he could get
tangled with.
his eye-glows hopped up and down with excitement,

and jiggled with his wagging tail.
he knows i can fix anything.

somehow big's cable had snagged on a small bush at the very end
of its reach.
there wasn't enough slack for us to get it loose.
amy suggested;
"do you want me to unhook him and then we can get it loose?"
"good idea."
big was standing in the rain, unattached.
"no need to stand in the rain big, go wait on the porch."
we didn't have to tell him twice.

when amy released him, the cable just fell loose.
so i still don't know what it was caught on.

when we reached the porch, big met me at the top of the steps,
leaned against my legs with his whole body,
and looked up into my eyes with his eyes fairly shining with
affection and gratitude.
it didn't take any special bond to read what he was thinking.

amy got a dog-towel to dry him off some,
and got the same treatment while she was toweling.
she spoke it aloud;
"i knew you'd come!"

we looked at each other feeling guilty.
we wished we were as good as our dogs think we are.

laz

09-11-12
close encounters of the big kind

me & big's favorite time of day is morning twilight.
(actually, i think big's favorite time of day is all day)
we still have the world to ourselves, with little to no human activity,
but we can see.
(again, with big's nose i don't think darkness is much hindrance to him)

the other morning we were walking up one of the hills on fosterville road,
with a pasture off to our left.
we were passing a stretch where head-high growth along the fence formed sort of a natural hedgerow.
we could hear some large animals moving parallel to us on the other side,
and i just assumed they were cows...

until a large shadowy form suddenly came flying over the top just ahead of us. a majestic, 8-point buck landed on the road about 15 feet away and everyone froze.
we stood that way for long seconds;
the deer looking at me & big,
me & big staring back.
we were so close that i could see his nostrils quiver.
obviously he was as surprised to see us as we were to see him.

i was proud of big. for a dog who will always struggle with a prey-response problem,
he has developed pretty good self discipline.
he never flinched...
even when the deer finally broke the spell by turning, running on across the road, leaping into the woods and disappearing.

the only evidence a deer had really been there was the trail of fresh, wet hoof-prints across the road.
we continued our walk, me praising big for his "good work" stopping for another moment so big could sniff where the deer had stood.

big gets plenty of practice on his prey-response control.
squirrels darting across the road in front of us,
short hares freezing until we are mere steps away before they
dash into the briers.
one morning we saw a mink scurrying across the road,
far from the nearest water.
the only creatures we come across that he cannot resist are the
cats.
he doesn't take off after them,
but he will pull at the leash and beg to be released.
big cannot understand why i tolerate nasty cats getting on "our"
road.

and of course the stink cats.
he will look up at me, seeming to ask;
"don't you remember what that stink cat did to me?"
skunk spray might be intended to discourage the next attack on a
skunk, but that approach won't work on a big.
he remains certain that stink cats should be eliminated.

we come across box turtles crossing the road sometimes.
we can see them from a distance,
their neck stretched all the way out,
and clumping along in the unique box-turtle version of
"hurrying."
(the further you stretch your neck, the sooner you will get there,
right?)
when they see us coming, they always stop to look,
decide there is no hope of beating us across,
and pull back in their shell.
big likes to stop and sniff them.
i used to worry about him chomping on one,
because he could easily crush a box turtle in his jaws,
but he seems to only be curious.

even when we are back lounging on the back porch,
the close encounters continue.
squirrels chase each other thru the trees,
short hares hop across the yard,
lizards bob up and down on the rocks, and make short dashes
here and there.
once in a while we can see a snake undulate thru the grass

(moving with surprising speed if they spy us watching)
big pricks up his ears and watches intently,
but he knows his job and stays where he belongs.

horseflies are a different matter.
if a horsefly decides the porch is a good place to hang around,
it is making a mistake.
big leaps to his feet and takes off in pursuit,
his teeth popping impressively as he snaps at his buzzing
nemesis.
if the horsefly doesn't decide to beat a retreat and head for other
parts, it is doomed.
big is relentless.

the other day a foolish horsefly decided big's butt looked like a
tasty treat.
i was sitting in my chair, big lay half asleep across my feet,
when suddenly a horsefly came zipping in and landed on his butt.
big was galvanized into action,
leaping to his feet and whirling around to catch the fly as it took
off.
the horsefly escaped the initial assault,
zig-zagging wildly, eluding the popping jaws of death by
millimeters...

a wise horsefly would have made a beeline for anywhere else on
earth, because anywhere else on earth would be safer.
this was not a wise horsefly,
circling around to come in for another try at that juicy big red
butt.
big was waiting.

the fly's intended landing spot on the big butt
was replaced by the popping jaws of death
(big is incredibly quick and agile)
and the fly was once again maneuvering for its life.
the fly jerked about erratically, making moves no fighter drone
could dream of making,
big was millimeters behind; "POP,POP,POP,POP,POP"
he caught the fly just enough to knock it to the ground,
and was on it in a flash.
unable to move in but one direction (up) the fly had no chance.

big snapped it out of the air, and flung it to the ground.
the fly landed at my feet and lay there, its legs twitching.
its body was severely dented.
big sniffed at it, carefully picked it up between his front teeth,
then dropped it again.
now, in addition to the dents, it was bent in the middle at a most
unnatural looking 90 degree angle.
big went over to his favorite spot to lay on the porch, and lay
back down.

a little later, another horsefly came buzzing by, and spotted that
tempting big butt.
once again, landing there elicited an immediate response,
and the horsefly found itself narrowly escaping with its life.
this was a smarter horsefly,
and it roared away as fast as it could go.
big watched it disappear into the woods,
then came over and checked his previous horsefly victim before
he went back to lay down.
i reckon he wanted to make sure it hadn't recovered and come
back to life.

laz

09-19-12
i never knew it could be like this

hello, my name is big,
and i am the world's luckiest dog.

i have everything a dog could want.

i have a safe, secure home in the woods.
i have a cozy bigloo with soft blankets to lie on.
it is a good place to curl up and sleep,
or just to sit and look out and watch the squirrels play in the trees.
i love my bigloo,

i have a master who tells me what to do.
i love to work for my master,
and he always praises me for my work.
even if i am not perfect he praises me after we work.
he knows that i always try my best.

my master never beats me.
once when i first became his dog,
i saw my master pick up a stick.
i remembered how my old master beat me
so i crouched to the ground and closed my eyes to wait on the
blows to come down.
i wagged my tail to show that i was ready for whatever my master
wanted.
if your master wants to beat you,
you must take the beating in a way that pleases your master.
master threw the stick away and petted me instead.
now i know my master will never beat me.

i have very important work to do with my master.
every day we must go out early and patrol our territory.
we have a big territory and it takes many days to cover it all.
after we get home i get to run and play in the woods.
master tells me to; "go-go-go-go-go"
it makes me so excited that i run as fast as i can go,
back and forth, and up and down the steps to the porch.
running thru the woods i jump over bushes and fly thru the air.
i love to run fast and jump.

when it is cool, sometimes i need to run with the little master.
it is my job to protect her.
i love to run and guard the little master.
even tho she is tiny, she is still very brave.
she is not afraid of bicycles.
i am glad she does not need to be protected from bicycles.
they are very scary.
it is my job to protect her from dogs and buzzards.

after i do my work i have plenty of good food to eat.
sometimes i even get special treats like fat or gristle or bones.
i am a lucky dog and i always have food when i am hungry.

but the luckiest thing of all is that i get petted.
when master and i are on patrol,
sometimes we see other people.
most of the time, they pet me.
when people come to the master's house,
most of the time,
they come out to my bigloo and pet me.

but my master pets me every day.
after we do our work he puts my food on the porch.
i am supposed to wait for him to tell me i can eat.
i love to have a master who is in charge.
after he tells me it is ok to eat i check my bowl.

if i have a special treat, i eat it first.
but before i eat my regular food i go to the master for petting.
my old master would sometimes pet me on my head.
this master and the little master know magical ways to pet a dog.

they do not only pat my head,
they rub my throat and scratch my chest.
they rub my ears and scratch behind them.
they rub my belly and scratch my butt.
you would have to be a dog to know how good these things feel.

my old master was good and wise.
all masters are good and wise.
even tho he took me for a ride one day,
and forgot me here in the woods.

i am glad he forgot me here,
because now i am the luckiest dog on earth...

i never knew it could be like this.

big

09-21-12
the big sun race

me & big are pretty consistent with our daily "runs."
we leave at the same time,
have a variety of courses of about the same length,
and we finish at the same time.

the sun lacks our consistency.
at summer solstice it is light before we get down the driveway.
at winter solstice the sun doesn't come up until we are coming
back up the driveway.
in between it is either coming up earlier every day,
or coming up later every day.

now me & big are naturally competitive.
big probably more than me.
every time a car passes going the same way as us,
big ends up pulling as long as they are still in sight.
he feels like we ought to at least challenge them,
not just shrug our shoulders and concede.
i haven't yet convinced him that we wouldn't stand a chance
against a car, even if i had two good legs and he had four.

fortunately we rarely see a car going either way...

except school busses.
now that school is back in session there are busses that pass us
on several of our routes.
every day we are doing a route that has a bus, we try to hurry
out, and move faster.
we want to get further before the bus passes us than we were the
last time we went that way.

the competition with cars and busses might be sporadic,
but our competition with the sun extends to every route we do,
and every day we go out.
now the spring end of the cycle isn't that motivating.
no matter how hard we try,
the sun comes up earlier and earlier.
we can minimize our losses, but we lose ground every day.
(sort of an analogy for life, huh?)

the fall half of the year is a different story.
we consistently get a little further before the sun comes up,
every time we go out.
success is a great motivator.

one of the big milestones, coming home from the east, is the day
we pass ben's bean field before the sun hits us.
(in the spring, it is ben's wheat field & we lose ground every day)
this morning we thought we had it.
where we turn onto the straightaway that passes the bean field
we can see more than a mile to the hills on the other side of our
valley.
we got a good early start this morning,
because we knew this might be the day
(our starting time falls within about a 5 minute span)
and we were moving at a good clip
(it took 16 days after finishing the bloody 11-w hundred before i
could move like i did before the race)
we got lucky & didn't run into any of big's friends along the way
(social obligations kill any chance at a good time)
so when we turned onto that last straightaway, the sun had not
yet hit the tops of the hills on the other side of the valley.

"i think we got it today, mr big."
i pushed up to my top speed,
which differs little from my standard speed.
big was more than happy to pick up his pace and stay with me.
we hadn't taken more than 5 steps before i saw the sun light up
the very top of the highest hill.
"it's on big, the sun is coming."
we pushed harder.

it is a long stretch thru the woods before we come out at the top
of the descent into the bean fields.
all that way we cannot see the bean fields...
but we can see the sun making its way down the hills on the
other side of the valley.
i never realized how fast it moved.

by the time we reached the drop off into the bean fields the sun
was halfway down the hillsides;
and it was still moving with remarkable speed.

the beans remained fully shrouded by the darkness,
but the trees that lined the little creek that paralleled the road on
the other side of the beans were now lit up halfway down.
"it's gonna be close, big guy. really close."

by the time we passed the trailer dog's place,
well into the beans,
i saw the sun hit the top of the tree on the other end of the bean
field where we make our turn.
looking across at the trees along the creek,
i could see the sun was almost at the bottom of the trunks.
i knew it would race across the field once it got past the trees.
"just a few hundred yards to go big. this could go either way."
we hammered on.

i was right about the sun.
once it hit the bean fields, fingers of light flew across the high
ground towards the road,
rapidly spreading out behind to fill in the low spots in between.

we were closing on the turn rapidly.
the spreading sunlight was closing on the road even faster.
the top half of my body was already in the light.
"we need a miracle big."

and we got it.
tall weeds along the east side of the road arrested the rapid
progress of the sun with us less than 50 yards from the turn.
it had conquered the bean fields,
but the road surface was still in shadow.

by this point i was hobbling along madly.
big was caught up in the excitement.
he might not be sure what we were racing,
but racing we were.
and big wasn't about to let himself be the weak link.
he hadn't even stopped to leave the trailer dogs a pee-mail.
(that's when you know big is really serious)

anyone watching our frenzied dash past ben's beans would have
surely thought us insane.

i could see the sunlight making its way across the ditch,
even as our turn (become finish line) crept up.
40 yards to go, 30 yards, 20...

and then, just as i began to believe we would make it,
the sun found a gap in the weeds.
in an instant a sliver of sunlight simply appeared on the road at
our feet.
it was no thicker than a pencil, but it was unmistakably a ray of
sunlight.
"we're beat big. it's all over."
one more step took us past the sliver of light.
"one more step, bigness. one more step."
it was that close.

we settled back into our normal pace,
and started the last long uphill haul to the house.
we might have lost today, but next time...

next time we beat the sun to that turn.

because for once, time is on our side.

laz

09-24-12
ding dong, the pug is dead

so the pug is dead.
i have to admit, i have longed for this day.
but somehow it is not as satisfying as i had hoped.

lynnor's nasty little pug had to be the most hated dog in short
creek.
it was the bane of all walkers and runners;
snarling and yapping, and trying to sneak in from behind to bite
your ankles.
everyone started looking for the pug as they approached it's
house,
and had to pass with their head on a swivel,
circling to keep the nasty little cur from sneaking in for a
cowardly attack.

it had a particular desire to get the big.
big returned its hatred in spades.
the hair down his back would stand up in a 4-inch wide strip as
we approached the pug house,
and he always stopped after we had successfully gotten past
to leave an angry pee-mail and kick up his biggest rooster tail of
dirt and leaves.
it eventually looked like there was a buffalo wallow on either
side of the pug's territory.

i was surprised to read that pugs have "good dispositions."
lynnor's little monster had anything but a good disposition,
and it challenged anyone and anything that passed by;
runners, walkers, dogs...
even cars, trucks, and tractors.

nothing discouraged the pug.
ben smacked it with his stick more than once.
i knocked it senseless with the trainer a time or two.
lynnor blasted it in the face with mace.
the pug was always there the next time you passed,
altho it became quite aware of the range of every weapon used
against it,

and threatened from inches outside that zone...
always trying to slip in when your back was turned.
everyone had their own pug stories.

the pug family was not indifferent to their dog's antisocial bent.
they would shout uselessly at the pug from their vantage point
on the porch;
exhorting it to "stop" and "come back."
the pug was indifferent to their entreaties,
and none of the pug family was about to rise from their positions
lounging on the porch.

periodically, as i was trying to keep the pug from getting at big's
ankles,
members of the pug family would shout for me too;
"let that dog bite him one time; that will teach him a lesson!"
i would respond that;
"i'm afraid that would be the last lesson he ever learned."

if the pug had reached big's ankles,
that would have been the end of the pug.
the pug could stay out of the reach of runners and walkers,
but big is incredibly quick and agile.
pugs are not.

if that fool ever got close enough to bite big,
big would whirl around and grab him before he could move.
and before i could stop him.
the entire pug would fit in big's mouth...

and that would be the end of the pug.
this wouldn't be like when little makes big mad,
and he knocks her down.
big hated that pug worse than cats.

how could i blame him,
i hated that pug just as much.
at the end of our driveway,
you can only go in one of two directions.
of the various routes we have to run,
half are out and back and half are loops.
do the math.
25% of the time we had to pass the pug twice.

another 50% of the time we passed him once.
75% of the times we ran,
we had to deal with lynnor's nasty little pug.

actually, there was some doubt that the pug could be killed.
there were rumors that the pug was in a league with the devil,
and could not die.

one day he rushed out to attack sandra's car,
and caught her by surprise.
she barely caught a glimpse of him charging out of the bushes
before he disappeared under the front of her car.
she looked in the rearview mirror to see him rolling to a stop,
ending up lying in a lifeless heap.

to her surprise,
when she approached the "corpse,"
the pug leaped to his feet and limped hurriedly away.
she left a note in the mailbox, apologizing for what she was
certain was a fatal accident.

no one saw the pug for several weeks,
and everyone rejoiced.
then one day the little demon was back.
the story went around that the mortally wounded pug had
returned to hell;
where he was reconstituted to return to his satanic duties.

another time he attacked a large dog which was neither
restrained, nor tolerant.
the pug took a terrible mauling.
i saw him afterwards and his little yellow skin had been
shredded.
his hide was laced with gashes, with raw meat showing thru.
knowing that the pug family would never take him to a vet,
i saw no way he could survive.
even a dog needs to have skin.

again the disagreeable little monster was nowhere to be seen for
weeks.
again we celebrated his demise.
and again he returned from his sojourn in hell;

neither wiser, nor with any improvement in his disposition.
but reconstituted in his original form.

the pug, the story went, might be immortal.

alas for the pug,
this would not turn out to be the case.
jeff, whose misfortune it was to live next door to the pug
(where the pug could come over to threaten him in his own yard)
came out one day and saw the pug standing in his yard.

jeff knew immediately that something wasn't right with the pug.
looking closer he could see that it was shaking violently and
frothing at the mouth.
while he watched, it turned and began to walk unsteadily back
towards its own house.
the little fool had attacked one thing too many.
rattlesnakes have very little tolerance for nasty pugs.

when it reached its own yard, the pug collapsed in a convulsion.
the pug family watched quietly from their seats on the porch.
he struggled back to his feet and stumbled on across the yard.
the pug collapsed a couple more times before making it across
the yard into the edge of the woods.
all the time his family watched in silence.
once the dog reached the woods they went about their business.

later they went into the edge of the woods and retrieved the little
pug's body.
jeff spotted it on the burn pile;
where they throw the household garbage into a midden heap in
the back yard,
and periodically burn it.

jeff told me this with a grim look on his face.
like the rest of us, he had no love lost for the pug.
however, as he said;
"damn. if that was my dog i'd have done something. i couldn't
just sit there and watch my dog die."

i only had one problem as jeff told me about the fate of lynnor's
pug.
"but i just went by there... and i saw the pug up on the porch?"

jeff just shook his head and with a tone of irony told me;
"they went and got a new one."

yeah that has to be it.
it must be a new pug.
he saw the old pug die.

i am glad the little beast is gone.
but the way it happened has left a bad taste in my mouth.

laz

09-25-12
big medicine

big can be something of an agitator.
i have told him that many times.
whenever we pass by the home,
or driveway leading to the home,
of another dog,
big always wants to leave them a pee-mail.
i understand the purpose there...

everyone needs to know that; "this is big's road."
when we pass by and the dog is there, barking and carrying on,
big is a pro at studiously ignoring them as we pass.
once past, however, he cannot resist the urge to lay down a pee-
mail, and then add an exclamation point by kicking up dirt in the
direction of the other dog...
peering over his shoulder just to make sure the message was not
missed.

and the message is never missed.
the other dogs absolutely hate it when big does that.
but the few who are not intimidated by big's appearance
have already learned that they have equal reason to fear my
"trainer."
all they can do is rage impotently as we go on our way.

i have warned big a time or two that;
"one day you will get a taste of your own medicine."
us masters know a thing or two.
and one thing we know is that what goes around comes around.

the other day we were going thru the hills over by fosterville
when i heard something rustling in the brush on our right.
i looked over just in time to see a big bobcat come out.
the wind was right, and me and big don't make a lot of noise,
so even tho he was very close,
he apparently did not notice we were there.

me and big stopped and watched as he leisurely walked out into
the road,
turned, and started walking down our lane ahead of us.

he passed within 10 feet of us.
big was so amazed he didn't move at first.
however (i don't know if i have ever mentioned that big doesn't
really like cats all that much... any cats)
as the cat started to saunter down the road ahead of us,
that was more than big could take.
in a split second big was pulling hard at the end of his leash.
"stop it, big"
i spoke low, and i hated to speak at all.
bobcats are common enough around here.
bobcat sightings are not.
and they generally last about one second after the bobcat
realizes you are there.
this cat was the closest i have ever seen one (alive).

this time was different.
the cat turned and stood sideways in the road looking back at us.
it was the biggest bobcat i have ever seen, tall and rangy looking.
his short tail had a couple of crooks, like it had been broken,
and he was twitching it slowly
while his unblinking yellow eyes glared at us balefully.
big had frozen on my command,
and now he seemed to be hypnotized by the stare of the cat.
maybe we both were, because i don't think we even breathed.

i didn't actually know the gender,
assuming it had to be a male because of it's size,
but we were about to find out.
the cat seemed to be sizing us up,
and obviously came to its conclusion about us.

i swear he had an expression of pure contempt on his face.
i saw the cat raise it's tail and the hind legs stiffen.
and had just enough time to think; "surely not!"
before he sprayed.
one, two, three big blasts right in the middle of big's road.
then he walked with deliberate casualness to the edge of the
road and with a couple of loping strides crossed the ditch and
disappeared into the underbrush.
(and nothing can simply disappear into brush like a bobcat)
when the cat hit the woods, his spell on big was broken.
big was furious, lunging at the end of his leash,

wanting to track that nasty cat down and establish the way the
pecking order worked around here.
big is the number one dog, and this is BIG'S ROAD!
his tormentor wasn't even a dog at all.
it was nothing but a nasty cat!

i let big "read" the cat's pee-mail.
but he only took a couple of cursory sniffs.
normally he likes to take his time reading the roadside news,
but he already knew what this message said.
and he didn't like it one bit.
big was practically begging to be let off his leash.
"did you see what that... that... that CAT did?"
big was so tore up that he didn't even leave a reply.
that's the first time i ever saw big at a loss for pee.

we walked a long way before big recovered his composure.
he was pulled up to his full height (short dog syndrome)
strutting and looking out into the woods and then back at me;
"there is some cat butt that needs kicking."

once he had finally settled back down i told him;
"so how'd you like getting a taste of your own medicine, big
guy?"
big never did answer. he never even looked up.
i think the taste was pretty bitter.

laz

fall 2012

hello,
my name is big,
and i love the fall.

in the fall the mornings are cool.
in the summer it is always hot.
the cool air feels so good,
i want to jump and run and play.

master always comes to get me in the dark
and we take our walks.
in the fall we can walk a long way.
we do not have to stop when the sun comes up.
i love to take long walks.
i could walk all day.

in the fall we get to walk in the woods
and the dry leaves crunch under my feet.
we see lots of animals.
i love to walk in the woods.

in the fall there are falling leaves
to snap from the air.
and campfires to sit beside with my master.

on the coldest days,
after we come home master will play with me.
i run in circles as fast as i can go,
and master shouts and laughs.
when i stop to catch my breath
master pets me.

fall is the best time of the year.
i wish it would last forever.

big

09-28-12
big time (part 1)

the temperature dropped into the 30's this morning.
and just like that, fall came.
sure, there is an official calendar date for the start of fall,
but out here in short creek, the real start of fall is the first cold
morning.

i had warning it was going to be cold last night,
so i already had dug out some warmer clothes,
and it was a good thing i did...

big was barking up a storm, creating quite a ruckus.
he was more than ready to start our walk.
the summer had been like a long stay in purgatory for my cold-
loving pup.
as i came around the corner, his customary greeting of "wooo
wooo wooo" came out in long trails of steam.
his stacatto barks of urgency punctuated the air with smoke
signal puffs.
i could read the smoke signals easily.
they said;
"HURRY HURRY HURRY!"

without warning he sprang high into the air in one of his
spontaneous leaps,
then i saw him gather himself.
is it? can it be?
YES!!!
he performed one of his amazing flips.

all summer long, i had not seen a flip.
he jumped around frantically whenever i came out to see him,
but the flips had seemed lost from his repertoire.
i had written it off to advancing age.
apparently it was just the hot weather.

as we headed down the driveway,
big struggling to control his urge to pull me into a full run,
i could not help but enjoy the brisk cold air pinching my cheeks.
i had always sort of hated the first day of fall.

i only saw it as a harbinger of the cold, miserable days to come.
looking at big's eyes, wide with excitement as he looked back at
me, there was no way not to share his joy.
it spread out around him like an aura,
engulfing everything within reach.
winter was coming, and winter is big's time.

walking our route,
i could not help noticing how much brighter everything seemed
in the crisp fall air.
i told big how much things were going to change over the next
few weeks. most of the year it takes a fine eye to capture the
subtle changes around us.
but spring and fall are explosions of unmistakable rapid change,
turning the pages between winter and summer and winter again.
today looked much like yesterday, much like two weeks ago.
two weeks from now the short creek would be transformed.

i looked across at the wooded hills,
still swathed in a blanket of green.
here and there was a smear of yellow,
where the early changing hackberries had gotten a head start.
a few worn spots revealed the nearly bare branches of the
cautious walnuts,
always the last to bud out and the first to drop their leaves.
in two weeks, those same hills would be a palette of brown and
orange, red and yellow.
only the dark green smudges of cedars would persist thru the
winter.

i looked around at the still green fields of grass and weeds.
then i heard the skree of a hawk,
and looked up to see his silhouette circling high overhead.
"big time is coming, huh mr hawk?"
in two weeks the short hares would be scrambling to find cover,
as the tall weeds turned into ranks of bare stalks.
every part of the year is good for somebody.
big looked up to see if i was talking to him,
then returned to sweeping his snuffling nose back and forth
across the road.
i still don't see how he can do that without scraping the skin off
his nose.

we came to ben's soybean fields.
they were still green.
normally they would already be yellow and ready for harvest,
but the early summer drought had set them back and they were
squeezing out every last day.
big & i walked into the edge of the field to look,
and sure enough, bright green pods could be seen thru the
leaves.
here and there a tinge of yellow just touched the top leaves.
in two weeks the entire field would turn yellow,
and then the leaves would fall off, revealing tall stalks festooned
with bean pods.
looking across the entire field was an amazing sight.
it had seemed impossible that any bean would survive the brutal
drought and heat of may and june.

there were some bare patches.
it was not the lush bumper crop of last spring's wheat.
but ben was going to get a pretty good yield.
the drought resistance of the engineered soybeans had surprised
even the farmers.

but, looking around,
the resilience of nature had been equally astounding.
back in early july, when almost all the trees had dropped their
leaves to save water,
we wondered if the forest would recover in decades.
most of the trees normally don't add leaves in the last half of the
summer.
they had proven more adaptable than i expected,
and only a scattered few had failed to refoliate once the rains
returned.
the insects had virtually vanished by july,
and the ubiquitous fence lizards with them.
however, while only a few of the hardiest adult lizards had
survived, eggs had been laid before the worst of the drought,
and a bumper crop of babies scurried everywhere.
by next summer it will be as if the drought had never occurred.

lost in our own thoughts, me & big finished our walk all too soon.
allowed to go leashless on the way up the drive,
big was bursting with energy.

finally i just told him to go wait on the porch.
i got a shower of gravel for my trouble,
as the big guy spun out like a drag racer.

when i got there,
i could see this was not just another summer day,
when big was content to flop down in the shade and pant.
he was waiting at the top of the steps,
looking down at me expectantly, his eyes twinkling.

i backed up until there was a sturdy oak tree behind me.
"you still have energy, don't you big guy?"
big sort of bounced on his front feet in reply.
"well how about we do something about that?"
he bounced again, and bobbed his head up and down.
"GO GO GO GO GO..."
big leapt to the landing in one bound and to the ground in a
second;
then he raced past me into the woods,
clearing me by inches.
i knew my job; i reached back and held onto the oak tree.
i learned long ago that it is all about trust.
as long as i don't lose my nerve and move, he won't touch me.
if i try to jump out of the way and guess wrong...

he will knock me tail over teakettle.
a second later big whooshed past on the other side,
and cleared the steps up onto the porch in one prodigious leap.
he whirled around and looked at me.
"GO GO GO GO GO..."
you have to see the big to understand the nerve it takes to keep
from flinching.
this hairy red giant bowling ball coming straight at me at
breakneck speed,
eyes wide, mouth open, tongue flapping in the breeze.
only to swerve at the last possible moment,
and miss me by millimeters.

he raced in and out of the woods.
he raced up and down the driveway.
he didn't bother to slow down to make a u-turn,
he just turned his body around, still going the other way.

and spun his wheels until he got enough traction to rocket off,
back the way he had come.
he skidded into right angle turns in front of me the same way,
feet scrambling as he skidded,
showering me with gravel as he got a grip and rocketed up the
steps.
every time he mounted the steps, he turned and looked at me,
waiting on me to signal the next round.
finally he stopped at the top of the steps,
and only looked back at me...

panting.

then he walked over and plopped down in front of my porch
chair.
"i think it is time for you to feed me and read the paper."

yeah. i used to hate the first day of fall.
and dread the long cold days of winter.
not this year.
this year i am looking forward to big time.

laz

10-16-12
big time (part 2)

Over the past couple of years,
time finally gained the edge in its battle with my dad.
Over that span he fought his way thru one crisis after another...
nothing less than you would expect from a man who had beaten
cancer time after time over nearly 30 years.

But each battle took its toll, and time is a relentless foe.
Each crisis seemed to fall a little closer on the heels of the crisis
before, and we all knew he was running out of strikes and outs.
During September it became more and more obvious that the
long fight was drawing to a close,
and as the month went on my time was more and more split
between our homes.
(I rather hope the backyarders don't discover some detail that
got lost during this time)

Luckily for me, I learned "conservative" values from him when
they were more about responsibilities than rights.
The big stories would have never taken place otherwise.
Altho he was an avid hunter and grew up on the farm,
where animals' ultimate destiny was generally the table,
my dad was a big believer in our responsibility to animals.
He always told me that owning an animal came with
responsibility.

"They are totally dependent on you. You cannot let them down.
If you own an animal, you make certain they are fed before you
feed yourself and you make certain they have shelter before you
shelter yourself."
His admonition that as a human we should
"never leave an animal to suffer"
was the reason that I brought that frightening monster of a dog
up to the house.

He also taught me the important lesson of compassion.
One day, when things weren't going well,
my dog came up to me and I booted him in irritation.
My dad immediately took me to task for it.

I pointed out that I "didn't hurt him."
That was not good enough.
"You don't have to injure an animal to 'hurt' it.
Animals may not be able to think like us, but they have feelings.
Dogs only purpose in life is to serve us, and when you scold them
or hit them, they always think it is their fault."

September was kind of a strain,
trying to keep up with the needs of my animals,
and still put in my stints sitting with my dad.
On the morning of October 2, we all knew that my dad's time was
measured in hours and not weeks.
I was at home and had just finished walking big when the call
came;
"You better come now."
I started to just put big on his cable and head out.
After all, missing one meal would hardly hurt the big guy.
Then I looked at the big; he was already up on the porch, "sitting"
and anxiously awaiting me to join him for our special time.
It hardly seemed a fitting tribute to my dad to tie the old boy up
and leave him.
So we did our usual thing;
big wrestling with the competing desires to eat and to cuddle...
as usual cuddling came first.

I cut him a little short, and when I arrived,
my dad was still hanging in there.
A few hours later he finally drew his last struggling breath.
And time won, as it always does in the end.
His family was all around him.
I don't think he would have asked for anything more.

laz

10-18-12
an empty place on big's road

so me and big went to millersville this morning.
it started out just like any fall morning in our little valley;
sunny and crisp, but not cold,
birds singing,
showers of leaves falling with every breeze.
it was the kind of morning that me and big just walk and talk,
and the miles go by without even being noticed.

it wasn't till we were on the return leg,
passing thru millersburg,
that i noticed the sign in front of millersburg church.
reading thru the leaves i made out:

"Resting With God
        Dorothy Ash"

i read it aloud to big.
"that can't be all of it mr big.
maybe it says 'guest speaker' on top."
i looked hard as we got closer,
but that was all there was.
"that can't be right. we just saw her last week."

dot was one of big's special friends,
and one of the regular walkers we passed on our rounds.
the first time we met her, she was terrified of big.

eying him suspiciously she asked;
"is that a pit bull?"
it was more of an accusation than a question.
after she continued on her way,
she kept glancing over her shoulder,
as if the hound from hell might be coming after her.

but ambassador big has a way with the ladies,
and it wasn't long before she would greet him with a smile.
we'd stop a little before we reached her and i would tell big to
"SIT."
and he would try mightily to comply.

he would squat, but he had a hard time actually getting his butt
on the ground.
and he kept popping up, only to be reminded to "SIT" until he
had permission to go and greet dot.
finally (after what i am sure big thought was an eon) dot would
come up even with us,
and i would give big his "OK."
big would strain at the end of his leash, tail wagging furiously,
until he got within arms length.
then he would bow his thick neck and present her with the top of
his massive head.
dot would reach out and pat him,
while telling him what a good dog he was.
he just seemed to understand that the big lean wasn't right for
dot.

we got to know dot pretty well during our little meetings.
after big got his petting, he would sit quietly and look around
while dot and i talked.
we shared a love of the woods and fields
and walking along our secluded roadways.
in her 80's, dot could tell us a lot about the way it was,
when little towns like millersburg and short creek were centers
of activity.
her husband was the preacher at hoover gap church,
the midway point of our temple half-marathon course.
it was never locked, and we were invited to use it as a water or
bathroom stop as needed.
dot was a valued member of the big team.

we walked on in silence, until we reached dot's house.
i stopped at the driveway.
"you know we have to go ask, mr big."

big was happy enough to go up to the porch.
we had stopped here to talk to dot a few times,
when we saw her out puttering with her flowers.
his tail was wagging as i knocked on the door.

but when the door opened, it wasn't dot.
her husband, a big man with a booming voice,
 greeted us with a; "hello big."

big nearly pulled me down the steps.
he was unnerved by this giant stranger with the thunderous
voice... who knew his name!
"that's a stout dog"
mr ash observed as i caught my balance and got the big stopped.

"yeah. he's part tractor."
i wasn't really sure what to say next.
"i saw the sign at millersburg church..."
"yes. dot passed away last friday."
"i was hoping i misunderstood. we just saw her last week."
"it was sudden. she walked her 4 miles four days before i buried
her. but that was the way she always said she wanted to go."
it struck me that we must have seen her on her last walk.
"you know" mr ash said, almost to himself,
"i preached at her funeral. i didn't want to, but she made me
promise. it was the hardest thing i've ever done..."

"i sure did love that woman."

we talked a little while about dot,
and what a good friend she had been.
big finally relaxed and came up to lean his head against me and
watch us talk.
you never can be sure what that dog understands,
but he looked awfully serious.
after a while it seemed like time for me and big to move on.

as we started down the steps mr ash added;
"you know, dot never did like dogs. but she sure did like big. she
was always telling me about him."
"big has a way with the ladies."
"well, thank you for stopping by. i appreciate the thought, and it
was good to finally meet big."

the road seemed somehow emptier as we continued on our way.
the trees along this stretch form a canopy over the road,
sort of a long green tunnel, turning brown and yellow as the
leaves have started changing.
shafts of sunlight penetrated creating a light show of bright
shafts ahead of us.
the birds were still singing,
but today i knew we wouldn't see dot's tiny figure come around

the bend in the distance.
and i wouldn't have to nag big to stop pulling,
while he pulled anyway, head high and tail wagging as he tried
his best to hurry and greet his friend.

there is an empty place on big's road.

laz

10-20-12
the big backyard ultra

in late october, big hosts his own ultramarathon race.
we have a 4-mile course laid out on the trails on the big farm,
and the way the race works is that we have a 4-mile race around
the course at 0700...

and we have another race around the course at 0800...

and 0900, and 1000, and 1100,
and every hour, on the hour, until only one runner is left.

crews, families, dropped out runners, and the big dog
sit around a campfire at the start/finish in the front yard.

it is a grand weekend for big,
with lots of petting and attention.

and it is a tremendous challenge for the runners,
as hour follows hour,
and the miles add up,
with no certainty of how long or how far
the race will actually go.

it has taken a couple of years to figure out how to run the race,
so that big can relax and enjoy the event.
and for the runners to figure out how to compete in such a
strange format.

these days it has become a big event on the racing calendar...

and a fun weekend in big's year.
this year is the second time big hosted the race.

laz

10-24-12
the big routine

things around the big farm were back to normal this morning.
i opened my eyes, and heard nothing.
then i swung around and put my feet on the floor.
immediately i heard the faint sound of big barking for me to
hurry up.
the big guy has become much more patient as he gets older...

he used to go nuts when my eyes opened.

yesterday his grinning face was peering in the back door when i
came downstairs.
he had gotten out of the habit of pretending to be restrained over
the weekend.
this morning he was still out on his cable,
and he waited there, albeit jumping around and barking urgently,
until i came to get him for our morning patrol.

big's backyard race weekend was a much happier experience for
him this year.
he has had another year to learn how to deal with challenging
situations, and we have learned a lot about making it easier for
him to succeed.
big had a wonderful time this year,
and he was really sorry when i took him down yesterday to show
him that all traces of the tent city were gone.

big didn't even suspect that something was up when we went out
for our walk friday morning. he was a little disappointed when
we took one of our short routes, but perked up when i told him
we would walk the trail later.

naturally big thought that "later" was when we passed the
trailhead going up the driveway.
bigs are not great with time.
later starts immediately after now in big's world.
all morning, while i was setting up for the race,
i kept wondering if big would take off his cable and come down.
he could certainly hear things going on...

especially when the truck that delivered the porta-potties got stuck in the front yard.
they asked me about turning around,
and i not only showed them where the rock was right under the surface,
but where the ground was soft.
they were not nearly as expert in driving that truck as i expected,
and immediately backed off the driveway onto the very exact soft spot i had pointed out...
with the heavy end of the truck.

big may have wondered what was going on down the hill,
but he was still waiting for me when i came up to get him so he could lead the course tour.
for a dog who feels the need to investigate anything new in his territory,
down to an empty cigarette pack or a discarded soda can,
the new stuff in the front yard was an overload.
especially all the people.
big loves people, but he isn't used to seeing that many at once.

but we knew how to handle the situation this time.
i sat down and let big sit between my feet and watch until he felt comfortable.
then he came out for a little petting.

when the course tour started big was pretty happy.
he was a little unnerved to start a walk with a pack of about 20 people following,
and he pulled more than he is ordinarily allowed during the short road out and back
(that section lets the field spread out a little before hitting the single track)
people were all fanned out across the road,
and he was afraid someone would pass him.
big is a great believer in things being in their proper order,
and big is the number one dog.
the only person who is supposed to be in front of him is me.

once we hit the single track, he relaxed.
all the people were strung out behind us in single file.
unfortunately, i made an error halfway thru the trail.

josh was doing a trial run to figure out his time checks for the
race, and we let him pass thru.
i knew big would pull until josh was out of sight,
but i forgot about that nose of big's.
for the remainder of the loop he had that nose to the ground and
pulled relentlessly.
he was sure that we could catch josh,
and that we needed to do so.
things were out of their proper order, and it needed to be fixed.
who would run rattlesnake patrol for josh?

but that was merely an inconvenience.
the real conflict came when i put big back on his cable up at the
bigloo and went down the hill to socialize.

now that big knew there was a party going on,
he wasn't about to cool his heels up there on his cable.
it wasn't 5 minutes before the big guy was coming down the
driveway sporting his ear to ear grin.

i was busy, so amy tried taking him back up the hill.
as often as he was returned to his cable,
he just took it back off and came back down.
after while she had to concede.

fortunately, all big wanted to do was to go from person to person
and make himself available for petting.
pretty much everyone obliged,
and he was the most contented dog on earth.

the friday night gathering was custom made for big,
people sat in a circle,
and he could make his way from person to person,
sitting down in easy range for a few minutes of petting
and moving on when it stopped.

me and big stayed down there until everyone had gone to bed
before we headed back to the house.
i knew big wouldn't stay at the bigloo unless he knew the party
was over.

saturday morning me and big were the first ones up and about,
getting everything ready for the start,

and then watching the gypsy encampment in our front yard
come to life.

big got a little more tense as people readied for the race.
i have found that the old boy is naturally hyperalert.
a sudden movement or an unexpected sound will cause him to
jump nearly out of his skin.
when he is around people, he wants to keep track of what every
one of them is doing...
at all times.

this is not possible in the chaos of a pre-race.
but i sat at the finish table, and big sat between my feet and did
his best to keep track of things, looking this way and that.
he was, at least, comfortable
and welcomed the people who stopped to speak or pet him.

as i expected, the start of the race panicked him a little.
it wasn't when the runners headed out,
but rather when they all came back...

apparently (in big's mind) all running right at him.
i was prepared this year,
and we were already halfway up the driveway.
big watched all the runners start up (after us)
then he turned and went into tow-motor mode.
he pulled me all the way up the hill to his bigloo,
i unfastened his leash, he ran inside the bigloo,
then turned and looked out.
he feels safe in his cozy home.
i put him on his cable and left.
my thinking was that he would be happy to stay in his bigloo all
day.

but my thinking and big's thinking were not the same.
after he calmed down a little,
he took off his cable and came back down to the gypsy camp.
obviously he was not going to stay put up the hill.

amy was good enough to go and bring down his cable,
and we attached him in the edge of the woods behind me.
this turned out to be a great choice of location.
all of the people action was in front of him.

he didn't have to spin in circles trying to keep track of 360 degrees of activity.
while i wasn't close enough to sit with, he could see me.
and he was only a few feet away,
so i could stop and pet him easily.

best of all, as each subsequent lap started,
he could go and lay under the truck out of the direct line of the runners.
big was comfortable enough to come out and greet the people who stopped by to pet him.

this worked out well all day.
i got him some water and food,
altho there was too much excitement to eat.
he also skipped all of his regularly scheduled naps.

for the runners, meanwhile,
the day settled into a regular cadence.
three whistles meant three minutes until the start of another lap.
two whistles followed, then one, and finally a cowbell sent them on their way.

the course was designed to be as easy as possible,
with no steep or long climbs.
however, there wasn't much flat,
and the rocky slopes of the big farm demanded constant attention and a certain amount of weaving among the rocks.
ultrarunners seem to enjoy watching video of runners leaping over obstacles.
in practice, they tend to go around things.

after last year,
everyone understood that there was no reward for speed.
the best plan was to finish each lap with as much left in the tank as possible.
there was no set distance to aim for.
the only opponent was the other runners.
the winner would be the only finisher,
when he (or she) was the sole finisher of the final lap.

last year some of the runners came with food to prepare,
only to find that there simply wasn't time.

this year most everyone opted for pre-prepared food that could
be eaten quickly.
the time between laps was deceptively short.
one poor runner was seen to put a pan of pasta on the fire
between laps,
and retrieve the charred remains an hour later, after the next lap.
he ate what he could.

a few runners had crews,
and to their credit the crews tried to help others.
but with all the runners arriving and leaving within a span of 10
minutes, there was a limited amount they could do.

almost every hour saw one or more runners drop out of
contention.
some failed to make the cutoff,
but most succumbed to a moment of weakness and failed to
answer the bell.
speed had limited value,
steadiness (both physical and mental) was everything.
the growing number of dropouts in camp became a ready pool of
defacto crews.

after 12 hours there were but a dozen of the original 29 runners
to switch over to the easy road loop for the night.

all went well for the big fella until the wee hours came.
the night had turned particularly cold
and eventually a dropped runner came walking up the driveway
wrapped in blankets.

the ever vigilant big,
who hadn't missed a thing all day,
spotted the apparition from a distance.
this amorphous blob wobbling down the driveway towards us
obviously presented a serious threat.

and big was ready,
barking a warning for the "blob-thing" to keep its distance.
for the remainder of the event big would alternate between
warmly greeting visitors
and warning the very same people to stay back.

the poor dog was kept on his toes,
as additional "blob-things" kept appearing
and wandering about the camp.
he warned them all.

big did not find my cavalier attitude toward the "blob-things"
surprising. i am, after all, omnipotent and without fear...
i'm not even afraid of bicycles.

the fact i would casually talk to the "blob-things" didn't mean
they were not dangerous to bigs.

meanwhile the dwindling number of runners seemed to grow
ever closer together.
at the single whistle, the survivors would emerge from their
various coccoons around camp
and assemble at the start line talking quietly among themselves.
there had developed a gulf between "them" on the trail,
and "us" in camp.
we did not, indeed could not,
understand what they were going through.

the longer the event went,
the closer the competitors seemed to become.
even though their only escape from this endless hell came with
the others quitting,
they seemed to be supporting and pulling for each other,
tied together by some invisible bond of shared suffering.

as morning approached i started to feel sorry for the big.
he had been up for nearly 24 hours.
that is something along the lines of 20 hours longer than he
usually goes without at least a nap.
so i put him in the truck to take a nap.
he lay down for a few minutes,
but then he opened the driver-side door and started to get out.
so i took him in the house and put down an old sleeping bag for
him to sleep on.
since i was going in the house after every hour to post race
updates, big was initially satisfied.
he stretched out with his chin resting on his front feet and
watched me.
his eyes immediately started to droop,

and within a minute his heavy breathing told me he was fast
asleep. but just because he was fast asleep didn't mean his ears
were turned off.

as soon as i got up and went back outside
big got up and followed me to the door.
i heard him bang on it a few times,
and when i didn't respond,
he opened the door and came to look for me.
it isn't always easy to have a dog who channels houdini.

fortunately he also minds pretty well.
i put him back inside and told him not to open the door any
more.
he didn't, but for the rest of the night he would immediately go
sleep when i came in to post an update,
and then come stand with his nose against the door when i went
back outside.

dawn was not only a landmark for me and big,
it signalled the return to the big trail for the surviving runners.
24 hours into the race, there were only three of them:
joe fejes, marcy beard, and andy emerson.
with 100 miles of running behind them,
they faced the trail with trepidation.
over the last few hours of the night loop, they had openly
expressed concern about being able to make the cutoff on the
trail loop.

emerson's fears proved well founded, as he missed the first
cutoff, leaving the race down to the final two.
fejes was the faster runner, but no longer by any great margin,
beating beard by only two or three minutes a lap.

reaching the finish, he would plop down in his chair and watch
anxiously back up the trail.
maybe this lap marcy would miss the limit.
each time she came in looking absolutely indestructible,
and a look of pain would cross joe's face.
at least one more lap.

after the sun came up, i brought big back out on his cable.
the poor guy was almost reeling with exhaustion,

but he would not surrender to sleep.
he had gotten pretty short on patience,
growling or barking at anyone who approached him that he
didn't think looked quite right.
at one point, a runner approached big and he backed away
growling.

another runner told him to; "go on ahead, he won't do anything."
i was astonished.
with big that has proven to be true (so far)
he has shown a total disinclination to bite a person,
regardless of the provocation.
but i wouldn't want to press the matter...

especially with a dog whose jaws could easily engulf a person's
entire head, or crush their femur.
fortunately josh was there to advise that one should never
pressure a dog that is backing away.

meanwhile, it was obvious that the end of the race was drawing
near...or not.

joe was still faster, but marcy looked as steady as a rock.
chinks were appearing in joe's stoic mask.
regardless, it was hard to envision either one ever giving in.
each was clearly determined to win,
but there was no mistaking the bond that competition had forged
between them.
whoever won would find not only exultation, but also sorrow.
there is a magical relationship between those who compete,
especially when the stakes are everything

one of these magnificent athletes was going to win.
the other would dnf.
part of me felt guilt at having made the parameters so
unforgiving.
part of me understood that otherwise they would have
succumbed to temptation and agreed to tie hours ago.
and this magical time would have never happened.

in the end, it was marcy who finally broke.
she started the 28th hour looking as invincible as ever.

but out on the trail she found herself unable to catch her breath,
her heart racing., and she had to come back.

when joe come running in, and saw her there,
his expression was of both joy and sorrow.
when he reached the place she was sitting they spontaneously
embraced.
they stood that way,
until we had to remind joe that he had to take a few more steps
before his victory was complete.
then they sat and talked for a long time.
the rest of us could only listen, and try to understand what only
two people could truly understand.

finally the last campsites came down.
most everyone scattered, except a few noble souls who assisted
as we started to take down the race site.
after a while we took a break, and i returned big to his bigloo,
where he collapsed into an exhausted and long overdue sleep.
while he slumbered, i removed the last vestiges of the race.

monday morning the big guy was waiting on the porch when i
got up, ready for our regular patrol.
when we reached the bottom of the hill, he stopped and looked
sadly at the empty front yard for a long time.
big had enjoyed a wonderful weekend.
i looked with him, because i had a wonderful weekend, too.
then we continued, back to our reliable schedule.

when we got back, big had his breakfast just like usual,
followed by some quality time on the porch,
until big told me it was time for his morning nap.
i took him out to the bigloo and attached him to his cable,
where he would pretend that he had to stay until i came and got
him...

because that is our deal.
things around the big farm were back to normal.

laz

10-25-12
the big buck

me & big saw eight deer this morning.
that wouldn't be so unusual,
except it is hunting season...

and all the local hunters have been telling me they haven't seen anything.
their problem is, they don't spend enough time in the woods.

me & big know where the animals are.
we go out every day,
and we make note of their habits.
we know where the turkeys are during turkey season.
we know where the deer are during deer season.
but we keep our counsel to ourselves.
we are not against the hunters,
without them, the animals would eat themselves into starvation.
but we will not betray our friends.

this morning we saw four does,
two bucks with at least 6 points, one with 8...

and the big buck.
he has at least 10 points, more likely 12.
possibly more, since we weren't close enough to count tiny tines.

we have seen the big buck a number of times.
we pretty well know his territory.
he has a fair sized range,
altho not as extensive as me and big's.
the big farm is right in the middle of it,
and that is where we believe he is holing up during hunting season.
him and his little herd.

we saw them in a bean field, off the big farm.
they have to come out to forage.
they passed thru a pretty thoroughly hunted area in between,
but me & big had already been thru there,
and there were no hunters this morning.

even though the big buck was furthest from us,
he was the first to spot us.
what a sight he was.
it is rare to see an actual mature buck any more.
he is a lot like big,
broad across the chest.
powerful shoulders.
and a thick neck supporting a truly nice rack.
he stood for long moments,
silhouetted against the morning sky.
i think he found it hard to believe that we had snuck up so close.

after a moment, the other deer noticed him,
and turned to follow his stare
(i didn't think deer were supposed to be able to do that?)
the closest deer, a little six pointer, was really close to us,
and he panicked first,
veering to get around us
(we were between the herd and the big farm)
and passing about 20 feet away.
the rest of the deer bolted when the first one ran,
and for a minute or so we got to watch them passing in front of
and behind us,
scrambling in a total panic
(they understand the implications of hunting season)
on their way back to the refuge of the big farm.

the big buck was not among them,
but when we looked back, he was also gone.
vanished into the air like a puff of smoke.
clever boy.

big was so charged up,
between the sight and the smell of all those deer,
it took 15 minutes to get him to quit pulling.

once he had settled back down, we talked about the big buck.
we know his days are numbered.
we never mention him to anyone local.
if the hunters knew he existed,
they would not rest until he was dead,
and they would go anywhere to find him.

we are pulling for the big buck,
king of the short creek forests.

big is the number one dog,
ben is the number one runner...
and the big buck is the number one deer.

i am not the biggest admirer of deer,
often referring to them as giant forest rats.
but i admire the big buck.
he is smart, strong, and at the height of his powers.
i am sure that no other buck around can match up to him,
and that the lion's share of each season's fawns are his.

i don't know how long a buck would hold the top spot in a true
natural environment.
most animals, like athletes,
are only dominant for a few short seasons.
but in this world, few buck deer reach actual maturity.
the big buck is an exception in every way.

me & big know the big buck's days are numbered.
no matter how clever, no matter how careful he might be,
sooner or later some hunter will get lucky.
and the short creek forests will lose their king.

for now, the three of us have a special kinship.
we know him and he knows us.
we will keep his secrets,
and he will surely keep ours.

laz

10-29-12
the great big day

we didn't get started before sunup today.
i did go out on the back porch in the dark,
the fact that big wasn't issuing his usual summons gave me a big
clue about what to expect.
the first thing i noticed was the rattling of runoff in the
downspouts.
the second thing i noticed was that it was cold.
wet, penetrating cold,
with gusts of wind pushing through the trees.
i took one look at the puddles on the back steps and went inside.

a quick check of the weather radar revealed bad news and good.
bad news for me, and good news for big.
a cold front was pushing through,
and the last of the rain would soon be past us.
i never loved running in cold, wet, windy weather.
even during my great running streak,
those were days that i did the minimum.
if it were up to me, i would have just cancelled today.
but coach big doesn't believe in days off.

i sat down to do some work on my computer while i waited on
the weather to improve.
i knew i wouldn't have to watch out the window,
and sure enough it wasn't long before i heard big start barking.
"come on out! the rain has stopped! it is time to go!!!"

bundled up, head to toe, i went outside.
by now it was light enough to see,
and what i saw was not encouraging.
there wasn't a low ceiling,
there was no ceiling.
the clouds were settled on the ground.
it wasn't raining anymore, but it didn't need to.

i tried to be in a bad mood,
but it was no use.
as soon as i saw the big,

and he greeted me with his "woooo wooo wooo" it was over.
there is no way to look into that broad happy face,
and watch that stocky body jumping around,
without feeling happy too.
he even did a couple of flips for me.

once big was on his big blue leash
(his favorite possession in the whole world)
we went down the driveway lost in our own thoughts...
big's thoughts were the happy ones.

when we got to the road, i turned into the wind.
"no way i'm gonna get way out there and have to walk back with
this in my face, big fella."
big didn't care,
he was busy sending a pee mail.

then on we went.
my hands felt cold inside my thin cotton gloves.
my cheeks felt tiny pinpricks from the larger droplets as the
wind drove mist in my face.
looking around,
the bottoms of the hills were barely shadows in the mist,
the tops were hidden.
a splatter of big raindrops showered us in passing.
looking down, i could see dark patches on the front of my coat.
"if i get too wet, we'll have to turn around mr big. i don't have a
coat that will shed water."
big pretended not to hear, and busied himself snuffling the
ground while we walked.
i watched the big guy walk
(he always reminds me of a big, red bear when he walks along
snuffling the ground)
i could see water dripping from his belly,
his huge front paws were flipping water on his belly while we
walked.
his back was dark with moisture.
i felt kind of selfish.
big doesn't have a coat that sheds water either.
i would have given him a guilty pat,
except that would have pushed the moisture into his downy
undercoat.

as long as it doesn't rain hard, and nothing pushes it thru, the
moisture would run off his outer fur on his back.
his bare belly doesn't seem to bother him,
but i sure wouldn't want to be out here with that cold water
splashing on my bare belly.

we passed by the pug house without the usual barking and
harassment.
nothing else was out, not even the nuisance dogs.
big left them a pee mail anyway.

we didn't see any short hares, no squirrels,
nothing was moving but us.
as we climbed up into the hills towards fosterville,
i noticed that my hands weren't cold any more.
actually, i was getting pleasantly warm inside my coat.
hills are good that way.

we saw a few stray leaves dancing across the road in the wind,
and i noticed how bare the branches of the trees had become.
the maples were still bright orange or red,
and the stubborn chestnut oaks were still green
(they won't give up until the frost actually kills their leaves)
everything else was bare branches reaching for the sky.
i noticed how silent it was.
the clouds around us seemed to soak up any sound.
not that there was much sound to soak up.
i had gotten used to big jumping when hickory nuts or walnuts
hit the ground around us.
and when one fell on the tin roof of a barn you could hear it for a
mile
the osage oranges had been falling from the bodoc trees for a
couple of weeks,
the large, green, brainlike fruits hitting the ground with a loud
thud that even made me jump.
scanning the trees today, there were no fruits or nuts left to fall.

we reached our turnaround in what seemed like no time,
and once the wind was at our back the walk was toasty warm.
the front of my coat hadn't gotten wet through,
so i felt confident the back would hold out on the way home.

"this was a pretty good idea you had, mr big. i'm glad i listened to
you."
big didn't say anything,
but i think he was smiling to himself.

the walk back was even better than the walk out.
big and i talked about the months to come.
i know he is looking forward to the cold weather.
a car materialized from the mist and went past.
the driver gave us a look as he passed that said;
"what the heck are you doing out on a day like this?"
i waved and thought to myself;
"we are having fun, this is a great day to be out!"

i thought i was glad that big had drug me out,
but the best was yet to come.
once we got home and started up the drive,
i let big off his leash, just like always.
(him being under voice control has been the best thing that ever
happened)

he started prancing around me,
looking at me with his face lit up, and his tail wagging.

"you want to run and play, don't you boy?"
big dropped down on his front legs,
his butt stuck in the air, tail still wagging.
"well, go do it!"
big took off, spraying gravel behind him.
he ran up the driveway until it turned,
then he stopped dead.
spun around and ran back as fast as he could go.
he disappeared down the trail.
moments later he flashed across the driveway like a big red blur
and disappeared down the other side of the trail.
i walked slowly up the drive,
watching my big fella running and jumping through the woods.
little runs through the woods like a pinball,
bouncing off trees.
big thinks he is a gazelle,
leaping obstacles and flying through the air with astonishing
grace.

for a long time, until we mastered voice control,
i felt bad that i couldn't run with the big guy.
he so loves to run and jump.
watching him play, i realized no one could possibly run with him
at the level he likes to run.
bounding over 4 foot tall obstacles and flying 10 or 15 feet,
landing on all four feet only to bounce back into the air like a
superball.
this is the most athletic dog i have ever seen.

we took our time getting to the house,
big playing, me laughing,
and both of us having a great time.
by the time we reached the porch (and big's breakfast)
he looked to be pretty well used up.
i underestimated the big.

after we had our quiet time,
and he asked me to take him to his bigloo,
i found out he was not finished yet.
like usual, he raced to the bigloo at big speed
going in the door at 90 miles an hour,
bouncing the bigloo across the ground with a thumping and
bumping, and emerging at the same speed
(i'd love to have a big-cam on him when he executes that 180)
to come over and get his cable attached.

then, instead of heading for the bigloo and his nap,
he ran to get the rhinocerous leg-bone his friend shannon had
brought to the backyard ultra.
35 degrees, with freezing rain and gusting wind,
just felt too good to go to bed yet.
he flipped the bone into the air,
and then raced in a circle around his area.
i neatly jumped his cable as it whizzed past, a foot off the ground.

around and around he went,
flipping his big bone in the air,
racing in circles, thumping and bumping in and out of his bigloo.
i just kept my eyes on the deadly cable,
hopping like a frog in a skillet,
showing my own skill at high-stakes jump-rope.

coach big's agility drills are the best there are.
you better get it right!

in the end, it was an exhausted, happy big that retired to the
bigloo for his morning nap.
i was pretty spent, and happy, myself as i went in the back door.
amy was sitting on the couch, doing some homework.
"man, what a morning!"

amy looked up at me;
"yeah, i could tell it was an icky day."
then she went back to her work.

i just smiled to myself.
no use telling her she had missed out on a great, big day.
it was a lucky day when that dog rescued me.

laz

11-04-12
big for congress

i already knew what to expect this morning.
we did this whole thing last year when the time changed.

spring is no big deal.
big has not the least objection to starting our rounds an hour earlier.
but the fall time change doesn't set well with big.
only our brilliant elected officials could truly believe they have the power to change the amount of daylight we have.
if i had the choice, i'd vote for big instead.
he is more practical.

i did get some good use out of my extra hour last night,
it was an extra hour to hull pecans.
i have a mountain of pecans this year,
and hulling them is a long, slow process.
i don't even eat very many of the pecans, it is sandra and amy that love them.
i am sort of hoping they'll show their appreciation by making me chocolate chip cookies...

i woke up with the sun this morning,
and i knew big would think i was an hour late.
we are supposed to be long gone before the sun comes up.
i was surprised not to hear him barking.
not a good sign.

i went downstairs and looked out on the back porch.
no big.
usually he lets himself off his cable and comes to wait for me on the porch when i am late.

i went and looked out the window to see if big was waiting at the end of his cable.
no big.
the bigloo was empty, too.
i wondered where my big fella could be.

i was a little concerned.
he has decided that he isn't supposed to go anywhere unless i am
with him, but i was a whole hour late this morning.
i hoped he hadn't gone out to patrol our territory on his own.
the neighbors all know him for what he is,
but any stranger that might see him would see an ugly,
dangerous monster, instead of a sweet, goodhearted puppy.

so i went out on the back porch to call for him.
i needn't have worried.
as soon as i turned the door handle i saw a movement in the
woods behind the house,
and big came running as fast as he could go,
bounding from the ground to the porch in one prodigious leap.
then he was leaning on me, wagging his tail and bobbing his head
with joy.
you'd have thought he had given me up for dead.

"i told you we'd be late this morning, big guy. it is daylight
wasting time."
big understands a lot,
but he doesn't comprehend time changes.
he has a clock in his head, and it says today is just like
yesterday...

and we are an hour late.

i set his food bowl on the porch table and went in to get dressed
to go. when i came back out the big was sitting next to the table,
looking at his food bowl and licking his chops.
he isn't about to eat until i tell him it is time.
big loves to have rules, and he abides by them faithfully.
i was sure he wouldn't mind waiting for breakfast till we got
back. big likes to take care of business before pleasure.

once we finally got going big was happy as could be.
the weather was cool and the sky was cloudy.
there was even a nice breeze to make it a perfect day for a big.

he was a little troubled when we passed the old johnson place.
there was a new dog on the porch.
we had been concerned after mr johnson had to move to a
nursing home last year.

big had missed him,
because he was often sitting on his porch
and me and big would stop by his fence to talk with him.
big misses his friends when they aren't around.

i was concerned, dreading the day bulldozers would signal
another beautiful farm turning into a subdivision.
we don't have any blighted areas in our territory and aren't
anxious to get any.
it was a happy day when we found out a family had bought the
farm, looking to have a place to hunt and fish and raise a few
cows.

when we reached the johnson place there were vehicles in the
driveway.
obviously the family had finally moved in,
and a big white dog was lying on the porch.
it sat up to watch us pass.
big's famous nose told him it was going to be there long before
we came in sight
and he walked along with his head turned,
studying the dog intently.

"don't worry yourself big, he's inside a fence."
of course, in big's eyes a 4-foot high chainlink fence isn't even an
obstacle,
but the heavyset dog on the porch didn't look like a threat to
attempt jumping it.

big still felt obligated to leave a series of pee-mails as we walked
on down the road,
and he kicked up a couple of impressive roostertails.

the new dog needed to understand how things work in short
creek. he was in big's territory, and this is big's road.

an hour later, when we passed by on our return trip,
the white dog was still on the porch.
not only was he not a threat to jump the fence,
he wasn't a threat to move.

comfortable that the hierarchy was established,
big didn't even favor the white dog with a glance.

after we got home,
and big had run and jumped and played,
then ate his breakfast,
he told me he was ready to go to the bigloo.
"no time for petting this morning, big guy?"
big just looked at me patiently.
i should know his nap was an hour late.

the new dog he could deal with, no problem.
i only wish big could accept every change with such equinamity.
of course a new dog that understands big is the number one dog
is one thing.
altering our schedule is quite another.
we have work to do, and it is supposed to start before sunup.

i may just have to start getting up a little earlier.

laz

11-05-12
the big absence

as we went around the corner, i saw big's head come up.
big drew himself up to his full 23 inches,
and walked on his tiptoes,
staring intently down the long straightaway.

i followed his gaze,
half expecting to see a tiny figure in the distance,
even tho i knew it wouldn't be there.

since dot died we have gone thru this every time we walk where
she used to walk.
where we used to meet her.
big misses his friend.
he is always sure she will be back today.

"she isn't going to be there, big guy."
big wagged his tail to acknowledge that i spoke,
but he continued to search up the road.

eventually he got discouraged and went back to snuffling along,
but every few minutes he raised his head to check again.
i wonder if he will always look for her when we come this way.

when i was in high school my dad lost the sight in his right eye.
at the time we had a bird dog.
after a couple of months my dad gave the dog to a friend who
lived on a farm.
i was mortified. how could we give away our dog?
we'd had her since she was a puppy.
my dad explained it to me;
"you and doug are teenagers,
you aren't at the point in your lives where you take a dog
everywhere, or have time to spend with her.
i can't take her hunting anymore.
those are the things that make a bird dog happy.
there is no need for her to lead a joyless life because we are too
selfish to give her up."

i knew he was right.

about a year later we happened to go to the farm where she
lived. i was sure my dog would be overjoyed to see me after all
that time.

she came running over with the other dogs when we pulled up
and got out.
they all sniffed at us, then went on about their business.
our old dog showed no sign of recognizing me or my dad.
she had a new life.
a happier life than she would have had with us.
i understood then, that dogs only remember people for so long.

big is different.
he had only been with me a few months before he moved to st
louis.
it was almost a year later when amy found him in nashville.
he nearly bowled her over in his joy to see her.
when he was brought back to us
he started wagging his tail when they pulled in the driveway.
our reunion was overwhelming
his entire body wriggled with pleasure...

of course, that is the same way he greets me now when i get back
from basketball practice.

i wonder if big is better off to not realize that dot will never be
there...

or not;
to get his hopes up every time we walk the dot loop,
and to be disappointed every time.

i guess i will never know.

laz

11-10-12
the big physics lesson

me & big were just finishing up our morning workout and
starting up the driveway
when we saw amy and sophie running up the road behind us.

i started to tell big;
"well, looks like you'll have to stay on the leash today."
instead i decided it would be a good test for the big fella.
could he stay with me like he is supposed to,
with the great temptation of amy and sophie following?
big's life is an endless series of tests,
and incremental improvements in his skill as a well-behaved dog.

big performed like a champion.
when i first took off his leash, he looked back at them.
amy and sophie started walking too,
when they reached the driveway,
but i told him;
"no, big, you have to stay with me."
so he walked along on his invisible leash;
poking around in the edge of the woods,
running a little ahead and waiting,
looking back to see what our trailers were doing.
but staying with me,
just like he is supposed to do.

by the time we got to the house,
the faster walking amy and sophie were only about 20 feet
behind us.

i was proud of my big guy,
and while i was busy being proud of him i forgot one thing.
one important thing.
we have been finishing up our walks with a round of bigsprints.
it does my heart good to see how much he enjoys his bigsprints.
before we had reached a reasonable level of voice control i had
felt so guilty.
he dearly loves to be able to let loose and really run.

when we reached the house, i told him "ok"
meaning (in my mind) "go on up on the porch."
big took off.
in his mind "ok" had a different meaning.
(i should have been more explicit!)

big raced to the porch,
bounding up the steps in two leaps,
then he wheeled around and came back down in one.
making a 90 degree turn in a spray of gravel,
he came flying at me.

mouth open, tongue flapping, eyes wide,
his face was a picture of pure joy.
as wide as he is tall, his body was a hairy, red bowling ball.
i stopped still.
i know the rules of bigsprints.
big will run directly at me,
but as long as i don't move he won't touch me.
it is like standing next to a railroad track while a train
approaches.
whooosh, the big guy whipped past me at about 60 miles an
hour.

i turned to watch him go,
and there were amy and her dog.
way too close.
they were in the field of play.
you don't want to be on the field during a game of bigsprints
unless you have nerves of steel
(and maybe are channeling evel knievel)
if you make a mistake, you are going to fly through the air.

poor old sophie is afraid of big as it is.
and that is without him bearing down on her like a runaway
train. she dropped and rolled onto her back.
big was past her before she could even get on her back.
he cleared the pair by inches.
amy looked sort of stunned,
like she hardly knew what had just happened...
except that she'd nearly been struck by a red, hairy, runaway
train.

big skidded to a stop 20 yards on down the driveway,
spun and, spinning out like a cartoon dog, started back.
sophie had jumped back to her feet,
and was really pumped up at the excitement.
if amy has ever taught her anything about the laws of physics,
the sophster has forgotten it.
she jumped out right in big's path.
this is sophie's game with big.
she goes to meet him,
and then rolls over on her back when he gets to her.
at 60 miles an hour, there wasn't time to think about rolling over.

so; back to big physics, do you know what happens when a 90
pound dog going 60 miles an hour,
hits a 50 pound dog standing still,
head on?

have you ever seen one of those toys with the steel balls
suspended on strings?
the one where you drop the ball on one end,
and the ball on the other end flies out?

that was what it looked like.
the impact stopped big dead in his tracks.
sophie, on the other hand,
went airborne like she had been shot from a cannon.

the fun hardly ended there,
because amy was still attached to her dog by a leash.
bringing us to the question;
what happens if you tie a 50 pound dog to the wrist of a 90
pound girl...

and fire the dog from a cannon?

when sophie hit the end of the leash,
she went down like a clay pigeon on a skeet range,
and amy flew off her feet like she was riding a broom.
luckily it did not just pull her arm off and throw it across the
yard.
i swear it got both her feet off the ground,
and propelled her about 10 feet forwards.

big wasn't even phased.
he just took off running again,
ready to start a new round.

sophie looked stunned.
i don't think she knew what hit her.

amy wanted to kill something.
i think she was trying to choose between me and big.

she's gonna laugh about this some day.
i promise you, she'll laugh about this some day.
but she wasn't ready to laugh about it right at that moment.
i made a point of turning away from her to laugh about it, myself.

and i yelled at poor big and sent him up on the porch.
his feelings were hurt, but it was for his own good.

let this be a lesson to all dog owners.
make sure your dog has a passing knowledge of the laws of
physics...

or keep them off the bigsprints field.

laz

11-12-12
the big choice

it was a rainy morning in short creek this morning.
for the first time in a long time,
me & big had to miss our morning workout.

we were still up before dawn,
and big came up on the porch to eat and spend some quality
time.
he was reluctant to eat,
because that would mean we weren't going on patrol,
but he finally did.
then he took his new favorite position;
i sit in my chair
and he walks up, puts the top of his broad head into my crotch,
and leans forward into me.
i have ready access to his ears and his neck and his cheeks
and that big hump of muscle on top of his shoulders.
while i gave him his favorite pets

i thought about how things had changed since the first time i
cautiously petted the top of his head.
that day i worried about putting my hand within easy reach.
doing the crotch lean this morning
he was one quick move,
one lightning fast chomp,
away from crippling (maybe killing) me.
we have developed a lot of trust between us.
actually, he has always trusted me.
i have learned to trust him.

once in a while he would break for a few minutes.
he would sit down, lean to the side,
and rest his massive chin on my knee looking off into space,
or sit up straight and look up into my eyes
(only for a moment, then he would look away. big is a very polite
dog)
devil eyes or not, big has a look that reaches into your soul.

i knew from the radar that there were breaks in the rain.
not enough to go anywhere, but there were some breaks.
so, when the rain stopped for a moment i asked him if he wanted
to go get the paper...

big is always ready for anything that includes the word "go."

i got my umbrella and went down the steps.
then i gave big his "ok" to come with me.
i didn't tell him exactly what sort of walk we were doing.
we have a number of different versions.
"rattlesnake patrol" where big walks in front of me on his leash.
"heel" both on and off leash.
i think everyone knows how "heel" works.
and the usual "do you want to walk off leash?"
where big goes ahead, falls behind, or runs into the edge of the
woods, while staying within a certain distance.

he looked at me, waiting for me to tell him what i wanted.
big always wants to do what is expected of him.
but i started out without giving him a command.
i was curious what he would choose.

to my surprise, big chose heel.
that is his least favorite,
because he has to concentrate on staying in position and
matching my pace.
i figured he chose it because that way he'd be able to see what i
wanted to do.
we have always done "off leash" on the return trip.
it's about a quarter mile to the mailbox,
and big stayed in perfect position the whole way.
we rarely do heel for that long,
and he usually needs to be reminded what we are doing if we do.
but he kept his concentration this morning...

even stopping in his correct position when i bent down to get his
paper.

as we turned to go back to the house, the rain started up again.
i opened my umbrella and told big he could go "wait on the
porch" if he wanted.
he didn't.

it was worth getting a little wet to walk back with me.
he did do the normal "off leash" instead of "heel."
he knew where we were going this time.

we spent a little more time on the porch while i read big's paper.
(he's the one who has a subscription...the newspaper lady loves
the big)
but his eyelids started to get heavy,
and he told me he was ready to go to the bigloo.
it was time for his morning nap.

by then it was pouring down,
so he ran from the porch to the bigloo.
i have an umbrella, so i got to walk.

after i hooked him up,
he sat in the door of the bigloo, watching me head to the house.
i looked at those big eyes, just watching me.
his expression was inscrutable,
but i knew when i went out of sight he would arrange his
bedding and go to sleep.

i thought about the latest article someone had sent me about a
pitbull ban in some podunk town.
they had codified the legends;
"pitbulls are bred to kill, and will attack without cause or
warning."

i wondered if maybe big isn't really a pit?
but then, he did fire sophie from a cannon yesterday.
maybe that's what they meant.

laz

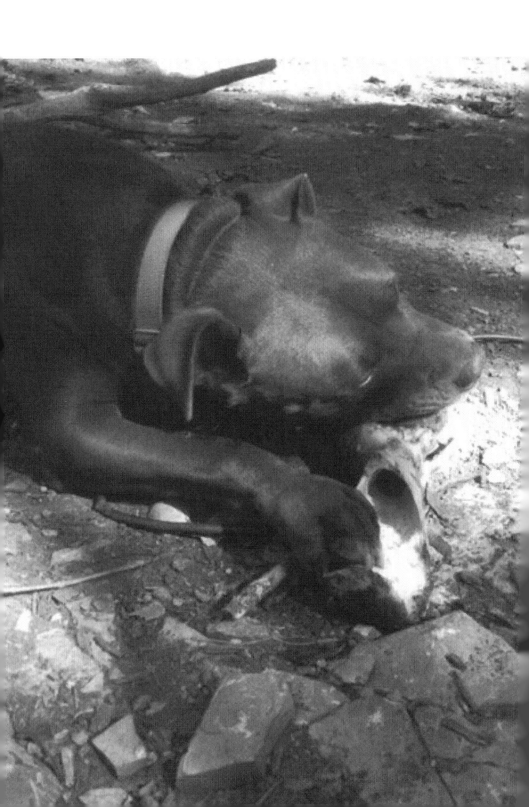

11-13-12
the big show

big didn't wait for my eyes to open this morning.
instead i awoke to the muted sound of him barking frantically.
"oh my god, it's almost daylight"
he seemed to be saying.

by the time i got dressed and came downstairs he was quiet...

no wonder.
he had removed his "dogproof" collar and was sitting on the
porch looking inside.
as soon as he saw me he "SAT."
"go get my collar and lets go!"

i wondered why he was so anxious this morning.
of course he did miss yesterday.
but he is usually patient even after one of our rare days off.
the rain,
which had signalled the end of a string of 75 degree days,
had been followed by plummeting temperatures.
it was about 25 degrees,
which big thinks is prime running weather.
but he is usually patient (in big terms, which means he waits for
me at the end of his cable) even when it is in the teens.

i didn't know what big knew.
there was a big show planned this morning,
and if we dawdled, we would miss it.

my first step on the pavement at the end of the driveway warned
me that we would be starting slow.
my foot slipped on ice.
"big. BIG. SLOW DOWN!"
with four huge feet and built in hooks,
big isn't troubled by the ice.
i was not particularly interested in busting my butt.
i didn't understand why he was in such a hurry this morning.
i didn't yet realize there was a big show planned.
and if we didn't get there soon, we would miss it.

as the light grew, i could see the effects of yesterday's weather.
the big drop in temperatures following the rain had triggered a
heavy fog...

which had frozen to everything it touched.
it had created a frost so heavy that it looked almost like snow.

the first special sight came around the next bend.
big hesitated, looking up the road.
following his gaze, i saw what had caught his attention.
the bright sunlight was reflecting off the top third of a distant
metal power tower.
the road ahead was still in shadowed darkness,
and the top of the tower was showing through a gap inthe trees
alongside the road.
it looked for all the world like a radiant figure waiting for us
beside the road.

had we arrived only minutes later (or minutes earlier) we would
have missed it.

as we continued, the light from the rising sun was working its
way down the hills around us.
when we reached ben's bean fields,
we saw they had been harvested since our last visit.
the big field at the bottom appeared to have been covered with a
white carpet. as we walked alongside, the advancing sunlight
flowed across the field to meet us, like an incoming tide.
for a few minutes the snowy white gleamed so brightly that it
hurt my eyes,
then the delicate crystals of ice began to melt.
all at once the field began to glitter with billions of flickering
points of light, set in the pure whiteness.
all the christmas lights in rutherford county would pale in
comparison.
and this incredible show was being put on just for me and big.

like so much of what we see on our daily patrols is fleeting.
a matter of being at precisely the right place, at precisely the
right moment.
"thanks big. you were right."
big didn't look up, but he wagged his tail.

he was caught up being fascinated by the stray soybeans that had
spilled onto the road as the harvest was hauled away.

the big show was far from over.
as we entered the woods i heard the plop of a big waterdrop
hitting the pavement beside me.
looking up, i saw that the "frost" on the tree branches had
melted, and now the water was falling back to earth.

we walked along listening to the gentle rain falling from the
trees.

we came to a small pond, fed by a wet-weather spring.
on the side where the "warm" spring water was bubbling up
under the surface a plume of fog rose into the air like smoke.
it was condensing back into water on the tree branches
overhead.
so much water was dripping back into the pond that it looked
like it was raining.
it was like a miniature display of the cycle of water that gives our
planet life.

tall weeds, their stalks soaked with rainwater,
had created cities of fantastic miniature ice sculptures.
me and big periodically stopped for a closer look at some of
them.
there were stalagmite-like towers climbing some of the stalks.
somehow the towers grow in layers,
forming stacks of thick rings with thinner necks between them.
i wondered how the ice formed in such a pattern.
did it come out in pulses,
somehow squeezed out by the process of freezing?

in others the ice was extruded through vertical cracks in the
dead stalks.
the ice had curved as it formed, coiling into rolls, some as much
as 4 inches tall.
in some of them, the ice was thick and white.
they looked like snowy cinamon rolls,
suspended above the ground.
in others the ice was as thin as a ribbon and translucent,
streaked with opaque white stripes.
i imagined them as some fantastic delicate confection.

i wonder how the forming ice manages to coil itself.
does one side freeze faster than the other as the ice squeezes out of the weed stalks,
or does it naturally happen when the molecules go from the random arrangement of liquid water
to the structured formation of ice?

or is there a simpler explanation.
"tiny ice men built these,"
i told the big.
he wagged his tail as if he believed me.
the ice sculptures were still protected by the shadows of the forest,
but as soon as the sun reached them, they would disappear.
"thanks for telling me i needed to hurry."
this time big looked up at me.
i think he was grinning.

we passed by dot's house,
and saw her husband driving up on his way home.
we see him pretty much every morning we pass this way,
for some reason i think he goes to visit her grave every morning.
("i loved that woman so much")
one day he will go to join her forever.

"the theme of the day is the fleeting nature of life, huh mr big?"

we walked a long way lost in our own thoughts.
then we came over a rise and i was looking at the forested hills ahead of us.
there were the bare branches of the deciduous trees, and the dark green smears of cedars.
scattered thru the woods were the burnt orange and brown shapes of the big old oak trees.

"do you know why the oak trees keep their leaves in winter, mr. big?"
big didn't answer, so i took that as him being willing to hear another story.

"when i was a boy, an old indian told me this story.
i think he told me lots of stories, but this one i remember...

there was once this young warrior.
he was tall and strong. well formed and handsome.
this warrior was in love with a beautiful young princess.
they were very happy.
but there was also in their village an ugly old woman.
she was evil and wise in the ways of magic.
she saw the young warrior every day,
and she wanted him for herself.
so one spring day she cast a spell,
and the beautiful princess grew sick and died.

the young warrior was heartbroken.
the old woman sought to console him and to win him for herself,
but she soon realized that she could never win him from the
memory of his princess.
so the old woman came up with a plan.
she told the young warrior that she would return his princess to
life, but at a price.
she would live until all the leaves fell from the trees in winter,
and then, after the princess was gone,
the young warrior would have to become hers.
the warrior was like all young men.
he did not realize how fast time passes.
and he wanted his princess very much.
so he agreed.

at first they were very happy.
but as the summer passed and the signs of fall began to come,
he became very worried.
the days of summer were growing few,
and soon his princess would be gone.

the trees of the forest are old and wise.
they see everything that happens, and they felt sympathy for the
young warrior.
the trees all talked among themselves and the oaks agreed that
this winter...this winter they would not drop their leaves.

the old woman was overjoyed as fall came,
and the trees began to drop their leaves.
but when it came winter, and the oaks still held onto their
crowns of leaves,

she realized that she had been tricked.
in a rage she climbed up into the oaks trees,
biting and tearing at the leaves,
trying to pull them off.
you can still see the bites she took out of the oaks' leaves to this
day.
but they held on, and the young warrior and his princess were
able to stay together.

and as long as the oaks keep their leaves in the winter,
the love of the warrior and his princess will live on."

i don't know what big thought about my story.
but by the time i finished we were almost at the driveway.

looking across the road i saw the big redtail hawk that had been
in our little valley all summer.
it was sitting on a branch,
high up in a big old oak tree in mr brothers' pasture.
but there was something different.
this time he wasn't alone.

a second hawk sat on the branch a few feet away.
as we stood there looking at them, one of the hawks took off.
it flapped its wings a couple of times,
and then soared in a wide circle over the pasture.
we heard his loud "SKREEE" as he floated thru the air.

i didn't look at the big.
"i know what you are thinking big guy. no way. that was just a
story an old man told me..."

"but it is pretty freaky, isn't it?"

then we turned and headed up the driveway to the house.

laz

11-16-12
the bone cycle

i went into sandra's office and looked out the window to see
what was happening in big's area.
(no one tell her. i promise i didn't touch her computer.)
i could see big's massive head,
lying on its side in the door of the bigloo.
the sun was shining in, and he was doing what all dogs love...

sleeping in the sun.

i could also see the little,
who had gone out earlier;
ostensibly to sleep in the sun on the back porch.
she was stretched out flat, straight as an arrow, motionless,
nose pointed towards the big, tail straight out behind her;
one forefoot hung in the air.
as i watched, she slowly reached out and carefully placed that
foot on the ground in front of her.
then, slowly, almost imperceptibly, her body oozed forward.
she was in full "stalk" mode.
her eyes never left the big,
but the object of her stalk was clear.
big's prized hippopotamus thigh bone lay on the ground about
halfway between them.

gradually the little inched her way across the space between her
and big's bone.
if he shifted around, she froze
and waited until he was still to resume her slow progress.

finally she reached the bone.
still keeping her eyes glued to the big,
she reached down and fumbled with the end of the hippo bone.
getting a secure grip, she suddenly jerked the bone up off the
ground, turned tail and beat it for the edge of big's area.
maybe the action scraped the bone across the ground.
maybe it turned over a gravel.
whatever sound it made, big heard it,
and he was galvanized into action.

the big exploded from the bigloo, bouncing it across the ground
as his thick body banged off the doorway on the way out.
little scooted for safety, outside the range of big's cable,
tail tucked, head held ridiculously high to keep the out-sized
bone from dragging the ground.

she made it by inches,
as big slammed into the end of his cable behind her.
content with being 4 feet beyond big's reach,
little lay down and began to contentedly chew on her prize.
big stared at her for a minute, his expression indecipherable.
then he looked at me hiding around the corner of the window.
"this is your fault. all that racket you make breathing and
blinking your eyes. how can i hear anything over that?"

big trotted back to the bigloo,
went in and lay down to resume his morning nap in the sun.

after a while, the little appeared at the back door,
ready to come inside.
"ah, so the thief returns."
i let little in and went out to return big's hippo bone.
it was nowhere to be seen, little having hidden it somewhere
(as usual)
but big had retrieved his spare (a caribou leg-bone) from
wherever he keeps it secreted, and was chewing away.

that night, when sandra let sophie out to do her business,
sophie made a find in the woods.
"sophie has big's bone!" sandra announced as she opened the
door to let the sophester back in...

"she wants to bring it inside.... NO, sophie... SOPHIE, NO!!"

sophie isn't particularly good at hiding things.
she left the bone lying in some leaves at the edge of the woods.
so, the next morning after me and big completed our rounds,
and he had returned to the bigloo,
i got his bone and took it back to him.

big looked at me curiously as i approached with the bone behind
my back. i held the bone up for him to see;
"look what i got, big guy!"

big pranced over to meet me, tail wagging.
i tossed his bone on the ground, and big pounced on it.
he picked it up, flipped it into the air, and took off...

there is no better way to celebrate the return of a stolen bone
than a game of "throw the bone in the air and run in circles."
i just laughed at my silly dog,
and concentrated on my own game of high stakes jump-rope.
agility drills are important for old guys...

at least that is what coach big thinks.

throw the bone in the air and run in circles
is a pretty demanding game,
so it wasn't long before big settled down for some serious
chewing, and i headed for the house.
it wouldn't be long before the whole bone cycle started anew.

i don't see how the little manages consistently to steal big's
bones, getting in undetected and getting out with both the bone
and her skin, but she does it.

sophie can't do it.
i have watched her try.
her first problem is that she doesn't seem to recognize the
importance of big not seeing her.
she trots over to his area like nothing is up...

like big isn't going to come running over to meet her.
at which point she collapses to the ground and rolls over on her
back.
big has come to enjoy the game of,
"push sophie in circles with your nose and try to turn her over."
i am not sure how much sophie likes her game of;
"stay flipped on your back at all costs, but try to crawl closer to
the bone if big looks away."
(and big does look away. i think he is distracted by me and amy
laughing at them)
i wonder if sophie has any plan for how she will get the bone out,
should she ever get that far.
we might never know, because amy always takes pity on the
poor girl,
and goes to rescue her before it happens.

big may can handle sophie,
but little has the mind of a cat-burglar.
little ends up with his bones several times a week.
and once she gets a bone, she is equally adept at hiding it.
i almost never find it in the same place twice.
most of the time, i can't find it at all.

lucky for big, the sophe can find his bones.
little can't hide anything that sophie can't find,
and the first thing she wants to do is bring her treasure in the
house.
"this time they'll let me keep it. i'm sure they'll let me bring it in
this time."

instead i return big his bone,
and the bone cycle begins anew.

we have some fun with bones inside the house as well
(you might not realize this, but dogs have no word for "share")
maybe some time i will tell you about sophie's clever trick to
steal little's bone.

laz

11-19-12
big steps

Me and big did the big trail this morning.
but we did it a little bit different.

we started out the usual way,
with big tickled to death to be on his favorite trail.
as always, it was sort of slow in places.
climbing over rocks and tree trunks with a dog on a leash is
hardly the easiest way to go.
especially with a dog built like big.

after we did the first jump, an idea came into my head.
"i think big is ready to do the trail off leash."
i wouldn't consider it on a public trail,
because i know what big looks like to people who don't know
him, but this is our trail, on our property.
big has proven himself under almost any circumstance,
and the only situations that would concern me would be;
1) coming up on a poacher with a gun, or
2) running into a cat.

i didn't think it likely big would approach a stranger,
and he would be within leash length of me, just not on a leash...
according to plan.
if he couldn't stay close, i would put him back on the leash.

and cats.
cats remain the one thing big can't seem to master.
the sight of a cat is more than he can bear.
however, i had no anticipation of running into a cat.
we have lots of coyotes...
and no feral cats.
that's the way it works.

so i put the question to the big;
"how about we take the leash off today, mr big?"
big just waited to see what i would do.
i took the leash off and coiled it up in my hand.
"now you gotta stay with me, big fella."
and off we went.

it was the best trail walk ever.
with big on his invisible leash, we could travel a lot faster.
it was better for the big, too.
if he came across an interesting smell,
he could stop briefly and sniff around.
i could just keep walking,
i wouldn't get 20 feet away before i heard big running to catch
back up.
he takes "stay with me" seriously.

i didn't have to keep an eye on him for when he was ready to
poop.
(and no walk is complete without a poop)
i noticed that he stepped politely off to the side of the trail.
not too far off, just the length of his invisible leash.
i waited for him to finish his business,
as that seemed the polite thing to do.

when we came to fallen trees, or big rocks,
the obstacles that require a little climbing over,
big stopped, just like always.
once i cleared, i didn't even have to look back.
i just gave the word;
"OK"
and i would hear the rustle of leaves,
or his claws scraping rock as he leapt
and the thud of his landing,
and he would be right back with me on his invisible leash.

we heard something running thru the leaves and stopped to look.
big cocked his head and pricked up his ears.
then we saw a couple of squirrels leaping thru the leaves,
engrossed in a game of chase.
they dashed across the trail behind us.
big watched as they spotted us and scrambled up a tree.
then he turned to continue.
there is no time to chase squirrels when you have important
work to do.

a little later a rabbit hiding in the leaves exploded out almost
under our feet.
me and big both jumped about a foot in the air.

we watched him race into a brierpatch,
then we went on.
big was more than justifying my confidence in him.

but i was taking him straight to the biggest test of all.
we were heading for the deer beds,
where the deer take refuge during hunting season.
on his leash, he always pulls there,
and wants to follow their tracks...
maybe even chase them.

i knew when we came to the first deer crossing.
big started sniffing the ground in circles,
and then he headed off into a cedar grove.
"you have to stay with me, big guy."
big stopped, and looked into the shadows.
then he turned and rejoined me.
and that was that.
i knew i had nothing to worry about the rest of the way.

we covered all the trails in record time,
and then walked some extra.
when we finally returned to the house the sun was already high
in the sky, and big was ready to get on his cable and take a good
nap.

"you are one smart puppy, mr big."
big's expression had to be pride, and he wagged his tail happily.
"you go take that nap, and i'll see you after a while."
big trotted off to lie on his chaise lounge and doze away the rest
of the morning.

we took another big step today.
and the trails just got a lot more fun for us both.

laz

11-19-12
more bone wars

dogs have no word for "share."
they have over 700 words for "crinkle;"
the sound that will wake a dog from a sound sleep and send them
running to see what there is to eat.
but they have no word for "share."

given that fact,
you would expect dogs to be very secritive with their few
possessions.
big is.
big buries his prizes, or stores them safely in his bigloo.
and big doesn't bury his bones like other dogs i have had;
scratch out a shallow grave, drop in the bone,
and carelessly toss a little dirt back on top...
leaving the bone half exposed.

big digs his holes deep, covers them well.
he studies the result to be sure that nothing is showing,
and even tamps the dirt down with his big flat nose.

he has even been known to camouflage his hide with loose
leaves.

little and sophie are the exact opposite.
their favorite game is;
"i have a toy...and you don't."
they flaunt their goodies in front of each other,

when little first arrived, it was just her and the old weiner dog.
the irasciblc old weiner lorded it over little,
taking all the goodies for herself.
sandra found that acceptable.

as time went by, little outgrew weiner.
eventually she realized that weiner could not keep her from
stealing toys any more,
and little started ending up with all the goodies.
thinking she had a solution, sandra brought each dog their own
small chew.

they each sat chewing for a few minutes,
while eying each other across the room.
then little swallowed her chew and went to steal weiner's.

little had a foolproof method for stealing weiner's bones.
she would edge closer and closer to weiner,
while weiner got progressively more agitated.
cranky, as many dogs her age are,
weiner would finally be able to stand it no more.
she would drop her bone and charge, growling ferociously.
little easily eluded weiner's charges...

because poor little weiner's legs were only two inches long.
little would dodge the charge,
then run around and steal weiner's bone.
weiner would pursue her briefly,
but she was old and soon out of breath.

sandra was incensed about weiner ending up without a chew.
her solution was to get a couple of long skinny chews...

obviously impossible to swallow.
wihtin 15 minutes there was only one chew,
and little was busy stealing it from the weiner.
we looked all over, trying to figure out where little had hidden
her chew, to no avail.
the mystery wasn't solved until the next day,
when i spent an uproariously funny half hour watching little try
to pass a foot-long rod of hard rawhide,

when sophie arrived, both her and little were still pups.
little generally won out by sheer persistence.
(why would anyone ever allow a bull terrier to breed with a jack
russell?)
little would then stick her prize in sophie's face, daring her to try
and take it back.

by the time they were grown,
sophie was simply the bigger dog,
and sophie always ended up with the toy.
she would then follow little around,
sticking the toy in her face and daring her to try and take it
back...

a risky approach,
since little would eventually find the prize unguarded and
swallow it.

in the end the obvious solution was to only give them toys when
the other dog wasn't around.
even the not entirely bright little and sophie eventually figured
out the routine.
at bedtime sophie gets her bone in amy's room.
as soon as amy and sophie go to bed,
little comes and begs me to get her bone down off the mantle.

the other night amy and sophie went back to amy's room,
and, as usual, little was begging for her bone.
near the end of it's life span, her bone was reduced to a small
piece of bone about the size of a half-dollar.
thinking it was time, i retrieved little's chew and gave it to her.
she lay down on the rug,
wagging her tail and chewing contentedly.

but amy had not yet retired for the night,
and in a few minutes she and sophie returned to the living
room...

where sophie was distraught at the sight of little chewing away
on her bone.
she lay herself down on the other side of the room, and watched
the little intently.
she didn't dare to try and take the bone away,
she knew how that would end up.
one of us would take the bone away and put it back on the
mantle, out of reach for either dog.

sophie oozed across the floor like a patch of black sunshine,
until she was lying with her nose mere inches from little's bone.
little chewed away in ecstacy.
the only thing better than having a bone,
was sophie not having a bone, and being filled with envy.
sophie just looked miserable.
periodically she would cut her eyes to see if i was still watching.
maybe i would lose interest and she could take that bone.

her sophie brain must have been cranking away,
because she suddenly got an inspiration.
she hopped up and trotted into amy's room.

we thought she had given up.

but that wasn't the case at all.
in a few moments sophie came trotting back in,
proudly carrying her brand new foot-long nylabone.
she went to the other side of the room,
and situating herself so that little had a good view,
began to chew away with relish.

little's bone must have gone suddenly sour.
she chewed slower and slower,
while watching sophe enjoy her grand prize,
until she finally stopped entirely.
she just lay there for a while holding her little sliver of bone
between her front feet, and watching sophie.

finally she abandoned her bone and started walking over to get a
closer look at sophie's.
obviously that was the break sophie had been waiting for.
she dropped her big bone like a hot potato,
and raced across the room to snatch up little's tiny fragment.
sophie flopped down and held her head high,
the diminutive shard of bone in her mouth.
her eyes shone with pride in her achievement.

little, meanwhile, took the big bone and lay down to chew in
earnest.

i had to laugh at sophie.
"clever girl!"
even amy had to laugh at her proud puppy.
"sophie, you goober. did you think this through?"

i have to admit.
sophie cooked up a brilliant plan.
but it was sort of like dropping a $100 bill,
in order to gain a fiver.

laz

11-23-12
the big schedule

big finally got in a run with amy yesterday.

after it turned off hot last summer, she had given it up.
big was always willing,
but once out there, he suffered so much in the heat
that she was afraid she might kill him.

once the cool weather finally returned,
she was more than ready to start taking him back out.
it is always fun to run with the big,
his enthusiasm and love of running makes it impossible not to
enjoy taking him.

but we ran into an unforseen problem.
big has a schedule, and an order for things, in his mind.
there are ways things are supposed to work,
and ways they are not.

amy's schedule has changed since last spring.
all last winter, i took big for our workout,
and when we returned amy took him for a run.

amy's schedule this fall forces her to run earlier.
and i was not that anxious to start our walk at 3 am.
i just figured i would let amy take big out first,
and me and the big guy could start a little later than normal.

he was plenty happy to see amy with his leash,
and everything started out fine.
i hid in the house,
knowing that if he saw me on the porch,
he would drag amy up the steps.

it turned out that didn't help a bit.
when they came by the porch, big drug her up the steps anyway,
and came to look in the door and see where i was.
obviously amy had put him on the leash to bring him to me.
our walk is supposed to come first.

big and amy run together really well,
but the truth is, that is only because he cooperates.
they are the same weight, but big is a lot stronger.

i went out on the porch to reassure the big fella.
"it's alright, mr big. you go run with amy, and we'll walk when
you get back."
his face clearly showed that he doubted me.
this was all wrong.

he went down the steps, then drug amy back up 3 or 4 times.
i would encourage him, and he'd start out again.
then he'd lose his nerve as they started toward the driveway,
and drag amy back.
he went to his petting station, and insisted on a hug before he
finally looked like he was going to go.
amy showed remarkable patience (especially for amy)
as they started and returned repeatedly.
i think her arm got longer on every trip back up the steps.

finally, we got the big guy to leave,
but as they went around the corner i could see him looking over
his shoulder, a worried expression on his face.
"this is out of order. without order, there is only chaos!"

i sat back to read the paper while i waited on them to come back.
i didn't have to wait long.
10 minutes later big came bounding up the steps, trailing his big
blue leash behind him.
he came over and leaned on me, wagging his tail.
then he signaled that he was ready for our walk.

about that time, amy came around the corner.
"it's not going to happen. he made it to the end of the driveway,
then he couldn't stand it any more.
he was coming back to the house, whether i wanted to go or not."

so big didn't get to run for a few days longer.
until the other day,
amy asked me if i minded getting an early start the next morning.
she wanted to take big for a run,
but we both knew things had to come in the proper order.

the next morning me and big hit the road extra early.
big's schedule *is* flexible enough to fit in an early start.
when we got back and amy came out,
he was overjoyed to see her,
as he always is.
(big loves his amy)
when she picked up the big blue leash he about wagged his tail
off.
he couldn't "SIT" to be attached quick enough
(this is a good way to sweep the porch)
altho it was hard to keep his butt on the ground with his whole
body vibrating with excitement.

they left without a backwards glance.
as they went around the corner i could see that he was wearing
his insane dog clown face;
the impossibly wide grin, and the whites of his eyes showing.
he was pure excitement at the prospect of running with amy.
he never looked back.

when they returned, he was a whipped puppy.
his first 10 miler of the winter had him ready to lie on the porch
and pant for a while.
he only ate a small portion of his breakfast before letting me
know he was ready to go take a nap.
by afternoon he was his old self again.
if bigs get sore, they don't show it.

so i suppose that any day amy is willing to take the big guy for a
run, i am going to be getting up extra early.

i don't want to see him miss a workout.
with his block of muscle design, he needs to be in extra good
shape if we are going to get in a 30 this winter.
and big deserves to be an ultra dog.

but there is a proper order for things,
and without order there is only chaos.

big is against chaos.

laz

11-26-12
big trail record set

me & big smashed our old record on the big trail this morning.

the old record was a mere 2:04.
me & little had knocked out a 1:56...

back when little was ahead of big on leashless running.

with big's new invisible leash, i knew we could break his record,
and probably little's as well.

big and i have been stepping up our mileage now that it is
cooling off.
i was a wee bit flat,
but felt like this was a good morning to "go for it."
even tho a couple of the harder days have left big laid out,
and we did a hard "run" thru the hills to fosterville and back
yesterday that flattened him.
he always recovers completely in a matter of hours,
no matter how hard the workout.
i have never seen him affected the following day.
i wish i knew his trick.

i knew we were making good time early on,
and felt good about making our ambitious goal of a sub-1:50.

i think every runner is familiar with how easy it is to keep
pushing when you know you are making good time.
big was amazing,
sticking right to his self-appointed place on my heels,
waiting for me to clear obstacles and call for him to follow.
he only stepped off the trail once...

to take his poop.
and that was on the climb between the fill lines and the hollow
oak tree.
i didn't stop to wait for him, but it was a good place to slow down
and let my leg get some blood.
maybe he planned it that way?

coming off the endless loop,
i started to think we had a longshot at 1:40.
that was a time that wasn't even on my radar when we started.
i could tell i was pushing at my speed limit,
because i started to clip my toes on rocks and roots.
as long as i didn't fall on my face, i supposed that would be ok.
even big was breathing hard
(it was over 40, so big thought it was hot)

we held focus all the way to the end,
and crossed the finish line together at 1:39:26!

we won't be running it quite like that next time.

on the way back to the house, big turned on the trail again.
"no, big guy. i think once is enough for today."
he didn't complain. just turned and came back to the driveway.

now we are giving some thought to big's first attempt at an ultra.
we can lay something out around here, and get it in,
but i think big would like to have an official finish
(so he could be a "real" ultrarunner!)

it might be difficult to find the right race.
it would have to be no more than 50k (30 would be better)
with a time allowance of at least 12 hours.
multiple loops would be best, for simplicity in arranging his aid.
the course needs to be roads/jeep roads
or some other venue with plenty of room,
so he wouldn't be in people's way.
no bicycles on the course (bicycles are tools of the devil)
lastly, the rd would have to be willing to comp big's entry as a
celebrity ultrarunner.
we'll have a hard enough time coming up with gas money.
big has to save his money for food!

if anyone has suggestions of a possible race,
me and big are open to suggestions.

laz

11-28-12
the other side of the fence

when the new family first moved into the old johnson place,
me and big thought they only had one dog.
the big fat white dog we saw the first time we passed posed no
threat.
the yard is encircled by a 3-foot high chain link fence that looked
to be well beyond his leaping capacity.
not to mention that he evinced little likelihood of getting off the
porch, or even standing up in response to our passing.

as it turned out,
the family has a veritable menagerie of canines.
in addition to the big white dog, they have a couple of tiny dogs...

actually, they could be mistaken for animated white mop-heads,
recognizable as dogs only because they make a yapping sound as
they run in circles.
they have no distinguishable features other than being
chihuahua sized balls of yarn,
the head end only recognizable when they are actually moving...

assuming they are not running in circles backwards.
i told big they probably had some cutesy name like;
"peekapoo" or "poohuahua."
the truth is, they are mutts.
me and big call them the tribbles in honor of the look-alike star
trek critters.

the last dog is the ringleader of the misfit pack.
and she is the biggest misfit of all.
somehow, someone managed to combine the most useless
features of a variety of breeds into a single dog.
she is grey, with black spots,
reminding me of an australian shepherd.
her coat splits the difference between a short-hair and a long-
hair dog; neither thick enough to keep her warm in the winter
nor short enough to be cool in the summer.
she has a long, thick body sort of like a basset hound, except
without the sagging, mixing the trim appearance of a hunting dog

with the girth of the basset.
her legs are as short as a basset's,
but instead of being thick, they are too thin for the body they
support.
her tail stands straight up at attention,
with the tip pointing forward over her back like a jack russell's,
and her thick neck ends in the small thin head of a herding dog,
except with large, bat-like, erect ears.

funny-looking to us,
she is the undisputed queen of the misfit pack.
the whole gang lives in an oversized doghouse in the backyard,
from which the queen maintains a vigilant watch.

they are usually all in the house when we come by in the
morning,
and queen bizzare comes roaring out first, barking furiously.
the rest of the dogs come tumbling out behind her like clowns
out of a clown car.
the queen tears around the house and out to the fence
where she runs up and down beside us, barking fiercely.
the fat white dog lumbers along behind and stations himself in
the corner of the yard,
(we are generally most of the way past the yard before he finally
arrives)
from where he sends pee-mails to big,
and kicks up roostertails in our general direction.
(i make big wait until we are past the yard before i let him send
his response)
the tribbles bring up the rear.
apparently incapable of running like dogs,
or moving a straight line,
they bounce along like furry superballs,
looping and circling, tumbling over blades of grass, bumping into
each other, and yapping like idiots.
i'm not sure they even know we are there,
but something is going on, and they want to participate.

the misfit pack is quite a sight,
ranging in size from 2 pounds (i guess, because who knows what
size a tribble is inside the furball?) to 150 pounds.

sunday morning we passed them on the way to fosterville,
with the usual greeting.
big, as always, was concerned that they would leap the fence.
since he could clear it with ease from a standing start,
i reckon he sees no reason it would contain other dogs.
i haven't been able to convince him otherwise;
"half those dogs probably can't climb the steps to get on the front
porch, big guy. none of them are going to jump that fence!"

but on the way back we had a surprise.
the queen had somehow gotten out of the fence,
and she was standing in the road watching us when we came
around the corner into sight.

i wasn't sure what to expect.
every time we walk past,
she acts like she wants to eat us for breakfast.

she wasn't barking, but she was sure staring at us intently,
as we grew closer and closer.
i could tell it was stressing her out.

a couple of times she ran over to the fence to look in at her pack.
then she would run back out into the road to watch our
approach.

when we got really close she wagged her tail uncertainly...

then she broke and ran back to the fence.
she stayed just ahead of us,
gazing longingly back inside the yard,
and looking over her shoulder to cast fearful glances at us.
leaderless, the fat white dog just looked back at her.
the tribbles were rolling around 'rasslin with each other.
forgive me for assuming the tribbles are pretty much clueless.
there was no fierce barking.
i had no idea how the queen had gotten out of the yard,
and i don't think she had one either,
because she was clearly searching for a way back inside her
comfort zone.
when she reached the end of her yard,
she went way back up the side of the fence to watch me and big
pass.

the big dog diaries

just before we went out of sight around the next curve,
i looked back.
the queen was standing in the middle of the road, watching us.

this morning we went by the misfit pack's house again.
they weren't inside their giant doghouse.
the fat white dog was lying on his back, with his legs splayed out.
the queen was curled up next to him for warmth.
the tribbles were rolling around 'rasslin with each other.

the queen spotted us and tore off , barking furiously,
to meet us at the edge of her yard and run up and down beside
us, barking fiercely.
the fat white dog arrived almost too late to send big a pee-mail,
and kick some dirt in our general direction.
the tribbles came bouncing along in the rear,
running in circles, bumping off each other, tumbling over blades
of grass, and yapping like idiots.

just before we passed the end of the yard i stopped and looked at
the queen;
"you're a lot braver on that side of the fence."
she stopped barking and stood looking back at me,
with her mouth slightly open.

i am sure that wasn't a sheepish grin on her face.
she's a dog...

that would be a doggish grin.

laz

11-30-12
the big cookie

i was late getting to my chores today.
i was supposed to get started cutting the brush that grew up over
the fill lines this summer.
but sandra had told me the cooks guy was coming for a termite
inspection,
and she wanted me to hang around the house until he came.
she worries about people coming to the house with big out back.

i could have argued that he is harmless,
but sometimes it is better just to go along.
(you know what i mean, sometimes being any time your wife
tells you to do something)

the intruder warning system (sophie and little) was on,
so i was watching out the back when the cooks guy walked past
the back porch.
he went on to the end of the house,
and turned the corner from which he could see big.
i heard big bark his greeting bark...

and about 3 seconds later i saw the cooks man return the way he
had come. he was not dawdling.
actually, he was moving at a rather fast pace,
considering he wasn't watching where he was going,
instead looking over his shoulder the way he had come.

so i put on my boots and went out to find the cooks man.
i kind of figured he might like an escort around the far end of the
house.

as i started down the second flight of steps a big grin started to
spread across my face.
it seems that little had stolen big's bone.
little had hidden it in the woods,
and sophie had found it, and brought it up to the house and left it
at the bottom of the steps,
where it was waiting for one of us to spot it, and return it to big.
the bone cycle is as much a part of our lives as the phases of the
moon.

cookie doesn't know about the bone cycle.
what he did know was that he had just stepped over an
enormous, thick bone
(did he recognize an elephant humerus? i do not know)
and something had clearly bitten it in half.
something like; well, like something really BAD.
who knows what could bite a bone that size in half.

the next thing he saw was this...

DOG.

this HUGE RED PIT BULL.

i know from personal experience that when you first see big,
his head looks like it is the size of a basketball.
and his mouth looks like it could engulf your entire torso or bite
a small tree in two.
god only knows how i would have felt if i had just seen a bone the
thickness of a small tree...

that had been *bitten* in two.

that "250 pound guaranteed" dog cable looks about as
substantial as a piece of dental floss,
when there is nothing between you and a strange big but that
and about 50 feet of open space.

i picked up the bone, to return it to big
(something that has become automatic these past few years)
and walked around to the driveway.

this time the grin got clear out.
the poor guy was standing next to his truck;
as close as he could get to the open door.
he had the look of a man who just wasn't sure what he should do
next. as happy as he looked to see me,
i think he was twice as happy that it wasn't the big.

"my wife said you were coming. she wanted me to wait for you."
i held up the half bone.
"i think this is why."
he just said;
"yeah... i noticed that."

his tone was flat, but i could hear between the lines;
"why on earth do you have chupacabra in your backyard???"

i accompanied him around the house.
big was waiting for us at the end of his cable;
with his "are you going to pet me?" look.
i don't know why everyone thinks that look means;
"i am going to take your entire head in my jaws... and pop it like a grape."
poor big.
he got the heart of a puppy,
and the face of a demon.

i went over to big and petted his massive head.
he leaned it against my leg and closed his eyes with pleasure.
then i bent over and whispered in his ear;
"i don't think he is going to pet you, big fella."
then i gave him back his bone.

big took it in his mouth, turned around and went back to lie on his chaise lounge in the sun.

cookie didn't hang around very long.
he completed his job, gave me the paperwork, and left.
somehow i suspect we will have yet another cooks man the next time.
i'm not sure why the same ones never come back.

laz

12-06-12
the big gift

i always have to laugh when people refer to big as a "rescue" dog.
most decidedly i did not rescue him,
altho he might feel that he rescued me.

i am at a loss to explain why,
but that dog decided at the very beginning that he was my dog.
maybe he could just tell that i needed a big in my life.
the vet was the first one to clue me in.
when i went to pick him up after taking him in for his bullet
wound,
she told me;
"these dogs are very attached to their masters.
and he seems to have decided he belongs to you."

little did i realize just how serious big was.
he needed a master,
and as far as he was concerned i was it.

that was my lucky day,
because whatever i might have done for big,
he has returned many times over.

and perhaps his greatest gift to me has been morning.

i have to admit that i never considered myself to be a morning
person. as a runner, it has fallen upon me to run early sometimes.
in preparing for special races,
i have even gone through some long periods of running early
every day...

but i never enjoyed it.

morning runs were drudgery.
getting myself out of bed before the sun came up a painful chore.
but that was all before the big showed me just how wonderful
the morning could be.
it is not possible to resist his exuberance at the beginning of each
new day.
the insistent barking that greets my opening eyes erases the

desire to roll back over and pull the covers over my head.
his joy at the sight of me with his big blue leash is infectious.
to start the day with big is to start the day feeling good.

one morning i realized that it was a disappointment to wake up
and find the sun already in the sky.
me and big are supposed to watch the sun rise.
every morning we head out into darkness,
and watch the world awaken all around us.
as the year passes, we watch the sunrise in its march from north
to south, and back again.
every morning on the road we see the darkness give way to light,
and finally see the world bathed, oh so briefly, in red,
as the sun peeks above the horizon.
while we walk the night creatures retire,
and we hear the world awaken around us.
morning is truly a wonderful time of day.
and by the time the other people begin to stir,
big and i have miles behind us.

peaceful, quiet miles of solitude,
as if we are the only ones to see each new day begin.
it is hard to believe i ever started the day any other way.

so no, the big is no rescue dog.
i am a rescue master.

laz

12-07-12
more encounters of the big kind

me and big have been enjoying this december warm spell...

actually, to be more honest, i have been enjoying it.
big huffs and puffs when the lows are near 60 degrees.
that doesn't curb his enthusiasm for going,
but it makes him work a lot harder while we are out there.

this morning i actually got to surprise the big.
his old tarp had served him well,
but old age finally got to it
and it tore during hard winds and rain a couple of days ago.
so yesterday i dipped into his bank account
and got him a new tarp.
this morning it was windy again,
and the new tarp was making loud "ripping" sounds as the crisp
fabric billowed in the wind.

i almost turned back over and went back to sleep when i opened
my eyes and big didn't start barking.
i thought it must not be time yet.
fortunately i looked at my clock,
and the glowing red numbers informed me that it was already
past 0430.
i hoped nothing was wrong with the big guy.

it wasn't until i got downstairs that i could hear his tarp
whipping around.
i felt pretty clever, drinking my apple juice in peace.
savoring it for a moment instead of gulping it down so i could get
out there before big had a heart attack.
and it was quite a change putting on my shoes without big urging
me to ("for the love of god!") speed up the process.

out on the porch, i could hear big sounds while i got his big blue
leash and my trainer.
they were scarcely audible over the flapping tarp,
but with long practice i could pick them out.
there was a distinctive "clink" as he stepped on a loose limestone
rock causing it to make contact with another.

there was a jangle/whip-popping sound as he shook his head,
causing his cable attachment parts to rattle together and his ears
to slap violently against his head.
i could even hear his cable drag across the ground,
scraping across sticks and rocks as he moved around his area.
poor big was at ground zero for the tarp sounds,
and he was clueless as to my imminent arrival.
but he knew it was about time, and he was ready.

i started down the steps; quickly speaking to the darkness;
"caught ya off guard this morning, didn't i big guy?"
i didn't give him a chance to be first.
"wooo, wooo, wooo"
came big's quick response.
then i heard his panting laughter;
"HAH-HAH-HAH-HAH-HAH..."
punctuated with heavy "THUMP"s as he landed from his leaps of
joy.
shorter intervals between "THUMP"s indicated when he included
one of his famous flips.
although the big was hidden in the darkness,
i could see his joyous greeting in my mind's eye.

then we headed out into our special time.
we watched the first light appear in the east and then spread
across the sky.
we listened to the valley waking up around us.
a chorus of caws drew our attention to the north.
i looked over to see three crows flying from the direction of their
roost in the woods behind ben's house,
heading out to forage for the day.
briefly i wondered if something had happened to our local
murder.
two birds are missing.
it is hunting season, and fools with guns sometimes think it is fun
to take a potshot at some crow.
then i see the two laggards hurrying to catch up.
our local flock is still intact.

big and i speculated about the huge flocks that sometimes pass
through. they do not mingle with our crows, and seemingly our
crows never leave with them.

"do you think that crows have different cultures, mr big?
are those just roving bands of young crows, without a territory
yet, or do they lead completely different lives?"
big just snuffled along the ground, reading the news about what
happened since we last went this way.
"i wonder how they percieve each other.
do our crows think of the others as gangs of thugs and punks?
do they resent the food those crows take?"
the big guy said nothing,
but i think he was considering my questions.
"and do those other crows look down on our crows as country
bumpkins? what do you think, big guy?"
big looked up at me and grinned.
running is more fun when you have a partner to talk with.

a little later we heard the "SKREE" of one of our local hawks.
the pair we call the warrior and the princess have been here all
fall. sometimes they are together, other times they are apart.
it is hard to tell if they are a pair, or just living in the same
territory.
the one we heard this morning was the warrior,
he was here all last summer.
the princess is new.
"you know, big fella, i think i am spending too much of my time
with the animals..."

"it isn't normal to be able to tell hawks apart."
the warrior's cry is distinctly raspier than the princess,
and his underside is more flecked with brown.
i knew it was him that we heard,
even though we didn't see him.
he was still resting in a tree somewhere in the woods to our east.
the calls were just welcoming the coming morning.

a little later we were startled by a loud "PHHHFFFF";
we had walked up on a deer and startled him.
normally they just stop and stare at us when we walk past,
but it is hunting season.
they don't like it when me and big catch them off guard during
hunting season.
hunting might only be a sport,
but for the deer the stakes are high.

watching the deer in the dim light,
trotting off with his white rump and tail raised in alarm,
i was reminded why runners should NEVER wear white during
hunting season.
moving through the brush at a trot,
the rump and tail bore a remarkable resemblance to a runner
wearing a white hooded sweatshirt.
only by concentrating could i make out the rest of the deer.

a couple more deer emerged from the brush to join him,
and the trio ran ahead of us before turning to float effortlessly
over the fence,
cross the road in a couple of quick strides,
and bound across the other fence to diappear into the woods.

big strained at the end of his leash.
i am never sure if he wants to chase the deer, or join them.
their graceful leaps remind me so much of big's own,
when he is running and playing bigsprints in the woods behind
the house.

not long after that, big became especially red,
fairly glowing.
i always know when the sun is right at the horizon,
because the reflection off the clouds casts a reddish tint to
everything...
especially the big.

but this lasts only a few minutes, and then the sun is up.

as we got close to our turn we passed by a driveway that goes
into the woods.
big always leaves a couple of pee-mails as we pass it going the
other way, so i know there is a dog,
although we have never met any of the people or dogs who
reside back there.

this morning big stared intently down the driveway,
and sort of tugged at his leash.
following his gaze,
i saw a man with a couple of dogs walking towards us.
at the same time, the dogs spotted us and started hurrying in our
direction.

strange dog encounters are not my favorite thing,
and i thought about hurrying down the road.
but the two dogs were too close.
nothing about our backsides retreating down the road would
improve the quality of this encounter,
so i stopped.
me and big turned and waited on the dogs to arrive.
i could hear the owner calling to them;
"SPARKY, STORMY, COME BACK HERE!"
sparky and stormy paid him no heed.

the dog that turned out to be sparky was a terrier type,
about the size of a jack russell.
stormy was just a "dog" of indeterminate lineage.
stormy had medium length hair, was a little taller than big, and
fairly stout. while about the same size as big, he was not nearly
as muscular...

and big's head dwarfed that of stormy.

both the strange dogs were males, so i was doubly on alert.
testosterone induced foolishness seems to be a common trait in
male mammals.
i watched the big closely.
he has a real knack for sizing up the intentions of other dogs.

big stepped out to meet them, which allowed me to relax a little.
in an attack situation he stays at my side until i tell him to get
behind me.

the other two dogs stopped on the far side of the road,
and went to post pee-mails at the exact same places big always
marks.
i might not know these dogs,
but big has been communicating with them on the doggienet,
so they are not total strangers.

the terrier was the first to come over and greet us.
he and big both had their hackles partly raised,
showing they were nervous.
it was not the 4-inch wide,
bristling brush that big displays when we pass the pug house,
so he was merely cautious; not ready to kill.

big has an interesting approach to the canine issue of dominance.
while he does stand tall,
he is unlikely to do any dominance displays.
he always assumes he is the number one dog.
i don't think any other possibility has ever occurred to him,
so he takes it for granted that other dogs understand.
the terrier was apparently accustomed to being a subordinate dog.
unlike many terriers,
he seemed to grasp the concept of relative size,
and he approached big in a clearly nonaggressive manner.

big and the terrier sniffed noses,
and wagged their tails cautiously.
by this time,
the older gentleman that owned the pair had gotten within sight.
"SPARKY! SPARKY, COME BACK!"
he sounded alarmed.

this time sparky was willing to comply.
he gave a little growl as he retreated and went to meet his master.
"see, i 'protected' our territory. nothing to worry about here."

stormy, on the other hand, had been waiting for the arrival of his master to bolster his courage.
as the man reached the end of the driveway,
stormy started across to check out big.
i smiled at the man and greeted him as cheerfully;
"hello! don't worry, he is not an aggressive dog."

the old guy was demonstrably unimpressed.
instead of answering, he looked at me with contempt (and fear)
this time the treatment big has to live with was extended to me...

as a "pit bull owner" i am subject to certain assumptions.

he did continue to holler at stormy;
"STORMY... STORMY... COME HERE STORMY!"
stormy could have cared less.

me and big might be the dregs of human and canine society,
but at least big listens to me.

stormy was hard to read.
up close i could tell that he was a pretty old dog.
his cautious approach spoke to his awareness that big is a
powerful dog.
none the less, stormy did have the fully raised back-stripe.
big was virtually calm,
with just a patch between his shoulders and a small strip near his
tail partly raised.
big and stormy touched noses without me feeling certain which
way things would go.
big was fine, but if the old dog was to bite him...
it was too much of a mismatch.
combined with the old man's urgency
(his "STORMY" cries were getting pretty high pitched by the time
the dogs touched noses)
i just decided it was time to move on.

i reached out with the trainer and touched stormy's nose.
"ok, stormy, that's enough."
stormy jumped back, looked at me, and went to join his master.
"there were too many of them, man. nothing i could do!"

i gave a little tug on big's leash;
"come on big, lets get back to business."
to my relief, big turned and we just walked on our way.

and so we had another close encounter of the big kind.
i would count it a success,
and i was pleased with how big performed.
still, i have half a suspicion that the story on the other side might
include terms like;
"near death experience", "vicious killer", and "lowclass thug."

while we regularly walk that way,
it is a few miles from our immediate neighborhood.
i can't afford to forget that not everyone loves a big.

the rest of our walk passed without incident.
we did see the hawk circling over the pasture next to the woods
where we had heard him call earlier.
"see, mr big. i told you it was the warrior. i think he's shopping
for breakfast."

big didn't look up, but he did increase his pace.
i think the only thing he heard was "breakfast."
i can't say i blame him.
we had a big morning,
and close encounters leave me hungry, too.

laz

12-11-12
big goes to basketball practice

big hasn't been barking as much in the morning lately.
if i don't get up soon enough to suit him,
he just lets himself off his cable and comes to wait on the back
porch.

i suppose i should scold him, or do something to discourage him,
but that winning smile, and that wagging tail...

big isn't just a ladies man.
he could charm the scales off a snake...

so this morning, it was raining.
it rained all night long,
and it was scheduled to rain most of the day.
big was already waiting for me on the porch when i got up.
he was soaking wet, but greeted me with his usual enthusiasm.

big knows we don't walk when it rains,
but we haven't missed a whole day in months.
we've slipped out before the rain, after the rain,
or even snuck in short walks between the rains.
once or twice we've even walked through a little rain.

big hates to get rained on...

but his work is very important.
he was sure i could work something out.

despite his entreaties
(and trust me, big is good at communicating what he wants)
we spent his normal walk time on the porch.
we talked, and petted, and listened to sports talk radio,
and when the usual time came he got his breakfast.

the morning wasn't a total waste, and big was happy enough to
go back out for his morning nap in his bigloo.

big even got a special treat.
tim came by to train on the big trail

(tim doesn't yet understand that running in the rain sucks)
and afterwards big came up on the porch to visit.
big and tim are buddies.
tim even got the rarest show of big trust.
big rolled over and begged for a belly rub.
when tim got ready to go,
the big treated him to a show of big sprints.
tim said;
"man, he is FAST!"
and also noted that;
"and kind of scary looking when he comes right at you."
fortunately tim knew the key was to stand perfectly still as big
roared past.

after tim headed out, i took big back to the bigloo.
it was a rotten day, and he didn't have a chance to play toss the
bone in the air and run in circles.
then i went in to get ready to run errands and go to practice.

when i came out to load the trash in my car to drop off at the
dump, big was waiting on the back porch again.
it had stopped raining, and big was ready to walk.
"look, the rain stopped. it is time to go!"
"i'm sorry mr big. it's too late. we don't get to walk today. but
we'll have supper when i get home..."

i went back and forth loading the trash while big waited on the
porch. he wanted to go back and forth with me, but i had told him
to "WAIT!"
every time i walked past, he wagged his tail.
and i reinforced the "WAIT!"

after the last of the trash was loaded i brought out a treat.
i had it hidden in my hand,
but nobody fools a big.
he promptly sat down, drooling,
and stared at the hand with a treat.
"you know you have to wait, don't you, big guy?"
big licked his chops and wagged his tail.
i opened my hand until he could see the treat sitting in my palm,
and held it out in front of his nose.

a long string of saliva stretched from his mouth, and dropped to
the ground.
(i need to taste one of those treats some day)
"OK"
my mother would have a heart attack to see me offer him food IN
MY HAND.
but the big is deft.
i barely felt his muzzle touch my palm and the treat was gone.

after he finished his treat i took him back to the bigloo...again.

i went inside, put little and sophie up, and locked the doors,
then i went out to leave.
big was sitting next to the passenger door of my car.
he looked at me and wagged his tail.
"i like to run errands."

"alright big fella.
you win.
you can go to practice with me...

but it isn't going to be as much fun as you think."

i explained the deal to big while we drove.
"after we run our errands, i have to go to practice.
you aren't going to be able to go in.
you'll have to wait in the car."
big just sat there, filling the entire passenger side,
and looked out the windshield.
big loves car rides.

he doesn't mind waiting in the car while i go in places,
altho he enjoys it even more when i take him in with me.
someone might pet him.
(more likely, they will recoil in fear,
but big keeps a positive attitude)
he has never had to wait for the two and a half or three hours
practice will require.
i was not sure how that would work out.
he generally spends his waiting time watching the last place he
saw me, waiting on me to come back.

i told coach mike i would have to go outside and check my car
once in a while during practice.
"i brought my puppy with me, and i'm not sure how he'll do."
then i added;
"i'm pretty sure he can't get out. it has a trickier door handle than
the truck...and i locked the doors. i don't think he knows how to
unlock it."
coach mike wanted to see this puppy.

after the rain, the windows were all fogged up,
but when i opened the door, there sat big.
he filled the entire doorway.

big looked out at us with that inscrutable pit expression.
coach mike said;
"that's one...*thick*...puppy."

"yeah. but he's solid muscle."
"i can tell...is he mean?"
"naw, he's the friendliest dog you'll ever meet."
big knew it was the right time to wag his tail.

by the time we went inside big had somehow wheedled a head
pat out of coach mike.

when we got home,
big was ready to eat and go to bed.
sitting in a car and watching the gym door for me to come out is
exhausting work.

laz

12-13-12
the big bone wars continue

i worry about the big on cold nights.
it is just something i cannot help.
somehow finding him waiting in the morning,
showing no signs of discomfort,
 does not seem to assuage my concerns.
the next bitter cold night, i still worry about my big friend.

i worried after yesterday that he might be getting footsore.
we did our usual 5 to start the day,
then he celebrated the delightful 19 degree morning with a
round of bigsprints in the woods.

then amy took him out for another 5 miles running
(completing a 15 mile morning)
while i took little for a few miles.

our weekly family mileage is pretty impressive.
amy got 15 for the day;
me, sophie and big all got 10;
and little got 5.
a 50 mile day is pretty good.

but big's unmeasured bigsprints were probably the hardest
workout of the day.
(you haven't seen speedwork, until you have seen bigsprints)

last night he seemed to be sort of stiff,
and big generally shows no signs of any effort.
so i wondered if maybe his feet were sore,
and told myself i would check them this morning when it got
light.

i didn't bother with it.
big has a recovery ability that every ultrarunner would envy.
when i went out to let him loose,
he was leaping and flipping like nobody's business.
big must have a whirlpool in his bigloo,
because he is always reconstituted after a night inside it.

the big dog diaries

i have changed my morning schedule.
now i get up and let little out to do her business,
then go let big off his cable to come wait on the porch while i
dress to run.
i might as well, because if i don't, he will just let himself off.
(if you can't beat 'em...)

it was another finger-aching cold morning,
so naturally,
big was still juiced up when we got done with our miles.
he raced up and down the driveway at breakneck speed,
while i was trudging up it at my old man pace.

as i went along he would run closer to the house on each round,
and turn further from the bottom of the hill each time;
his bigsprint laps following me up the driveway.

when we got close enough for him to go behind the house,
he raced across his favorite bone.
little must have stolen it yesterday and hid it in the woods.
sophie found it while we were out,
and brought it up to the house.

even at 100 miles an hour big smelled or saw his bone as he went
past it, and immediately skidded to a stop,
turned,
and ran back to look at it.
he studied his bone for a minute.
that big brain was humming;
then he grabbed it up and ran off into the woods.

i was expecting him to stop and chew it somewhere,
so i watched carefully.
i planned to go and retrieve it for him after he had breakfast.
instead, the big fella raced to the base of a big cedar tree and
started digging. after he got a suitable hole excavated, he
dropped in the bone and scratched the dirt back on top.
he stopped a couple of times to study his work, then scraped up
more dirt, until he was finally satisfied that no trace of the bone
was visible. then he took his broad nose and pushed dead leaves
on top, stopping periodically to tamp them down with the end of
his nose, until even i couldn't tell where he had been working.

big studied his handiwork carefully,
and made a few adjustments
(where he must not have thought it was perfect)
then he came on back for breakfast.

afterwards, when i took him back out to the bigloo,
i got a hippo femur that i had retrieved yesterday
(not his favorite bone, but certainly a good one)
i want to see if sophie can ferret out big's hiding spot by
tomorrow.

meanwhile, as we walked back to the bigloo,
the big was still bursting with energy.
he ran back and forth past me,
accelerating in two steps and then leaping as high as my head as
he passed his bone, screeching to a halt and whirling to go back
past me the same way.

when we reached his cable he sat down quickly,
his wagging tail sweeping the ground.
i hooked his cable on and held the bone in front of his nose.
his tail wagged even harder.

"OK!"

big took the bone carefully in the middle,
and when i let go, he tossed it in the air with a flip of his head...
and started tearing around in circles.
i left him jumping and running and tossing his bone.
it would seem we had not quite killed him yesterday.

this afternoon, little and i were outside.
i saw that big had brought out his sleeping bag
and spread it in front of the bigloo.
it made a soft place to lie while he chewed his hippo femur.
when he saw us, big stopped to come out and say hello.
naturally little got there first (i *always* bring up the rear)
big greeted her with wagging tail and they sniffed noses.
big was interested in little,
but i could see what little was focused on.
big had lain his bone in the doorway of the bigloo
i suppose that seemed like the safest spot,
but no place is safe from the little.

as big turned his attention to me,
little walked on innocently.
as soon as she passed the big, she took off for his bone.
bless his big heart.
big was too interested in me to notice,
so i hollered at little;
"STOP IT LITTLE!"
little was too intent on the bone to pay attention to me.
she was trying to get a grip so she could run with it.
"LEAVE BIG'S BONE ALONE!"
i took a couple of steps towards little.
i wasn't thinking clearly.
big turned to go with me,
and immediately spotted the little with his bone.
do you know how long it takes a big to hit top speed?
one stride.
little wasn't paying attention to me.
she was watching the big.
when he saw her,
she abandoned efforts to get the bone and took off running.
lucky for me, i thought quick.
i jumped before i even looked to see where the cable was.
i saw the cable whip past under one foot,
not quite under the other.
it barely clipped my right foot,
jerking that leg out from under me.

little was even luckier.
my weight slowed the big enough for her to escape.
i managed to bring my left foot down in front of me,
as the cable slipped off the toe of my right shoe.
stumbling and flailing my arms,
i managed to catch my balance and not fall on my face...this time.

i don't know how much rich pays for that gym
where he does those proprioception exercises,
but i'd be willing to rent him a big and a little.

it is a lot more exciting when you don't know the workout is
coming.

laz

12-19-12
big's bad day

yesterday was a bad day for the big...

actually, he thought it was a pretty good day before it was over.
but it sure started out like a bad day.

to begin with, it was raining again.
it had been raining for 3 days, and it was messing up big's life.
heavy winds and rain had attacked his new tarp with a
vengeance.

i had done the best i could,
repairing it between storms.
but one of the corner grommets had finally been ripped out,
and after that his dry space was doomed to gradually shrink
away.

sure, we had managed to get in his walks,
squeezing one in between rain storms,
cutting one short,
and just walking in the rain once.
but it was too muddy for any big games.
and there was no sun to lay in and sleep.

i spent as much time with him on the porch as i could afford,
but after we had been worked up to 60 mile weeks,
big was not happy to spend most of his days trapped in the
bigloo.

and now this.
it was raining harder than ever,
and i was not up to taking him for a walk anyway.

big did his best to convince me.
i heard him barking and barking through the sounds of pouring
rain.
when the barking stopped, i knew what was coming.
a minute later he showed up on the porch with no collar on.

i went out to find my big ugly dog soaked to the skin.
then, just as i had always been told would happen,
big turned on me without warning...

it was horrible.
it was a nightmare.
the sun wasn't up yet, and his pupils filled his whole eyes.
when he sat down and looked up at me with those sad puppy
eyes, it about ripped my heart out.

i had no choice.
i went and got his breakfast and turned on sports talk radio.

we sat there for about an hour while big dried out.
but he didn't want to eat.
he just sat and looked up at me.
because big wasn't having the bad day.
i was...

and a big always knows.
i didn't feel good and big thought it was his duty to sit with me.

i finally had to take him back to the bigloo.
i needed to go inside and lie down.
so i took him to his bigloo and told him sternly not to take off his
collar again.
it wasn't safe to leave him on the porch unattended.

sometimes, not often, but sometimes,
people come up to the house.
and no matter how gentle his heart,
big scares people.
my first duty to big is to protect him.

i found i couldn't rest.
maybe i am like the big,
and i know when something isn't right.

i went quietly into sandra's office and peeked out the window.

big was standing in the rain at the end of his cable.
as close as he could get to the back porch.
he could have easily taken off his collar and got out of the rain.
but i had told him not to.

then, as if i wasn't already feeling guilty enough,
he heaved a big sigh, lay down in the mud...

and stuck one hind leg out towards the porch.
it was as close as he could get to me.

is there no limit to how vicious these dogs can be?

i knew i had to find a better solution.
i went and stole little's bed out of the utility room,
and lay it on the porch next to the back door,
where big could look in.
then i went and got my big friend.

he was ecstatic.
no matter how bad you treat a dog,
they treat the least kindness as if it were the grandest favor a dog
ever received.
if big could lie in the mud for me,
i could lie on my recliner for him.
i don't think the sacrifice in comfort really compares,
and the recliner is next to the door so that big could look in and
see me. that was all he really wanted.
and i would be there close by if anything happened.

that is how we spent the day.
once in a while i would look out the door.
big would rise up and look back.
bigs always know.
i'm sure he could hear my eyes open.
it's a piece of cake at that range.

by the late afternoon i was feeling a lot better.
there was a break in the rain
and i went out and spent some time with the big.

the poor fella had been waiting on me to tell him it was "OK" to
get off the porch to pee!
after some talking and petting he was ready to eat.
once he had a full belly,
it wasn't long before i saw his eyes starting to get heavy.
big had missed his scheduled naps while keeping his daylong
vigil.

"don't you think it is about time for you to go to the bigloo and
get some sleep, mr big?"
big looked at me.
then he looked at his new bed next to the door.
then he looked back at me.
don't try to tell me bigs can't talk.

"no, big fella. i'm afraid you need to sleep in the bigloo."
big got up and walked over to the steps.
we walked out to the bigloo together and i attached him to his
cable.
"you get a good sleep mr. big, and i promise we'll walk
tomorrow. the rain is ending tonight."

we took that walk this morning, and it was a good one.
big had a grand old time.
sure he had a bad day.
but that was yesterday.

laz

12-19-12
the big christmas card

so, we were all sitting here in the house.
i was working on my vol-state book.
amy was probably twitting, or texting,
or whatever she does with that little device of hers.
sandra was bustling around performing random tasks,
when suddenly an idea popped into sandra's head.

this is not the first time an idea has popped into sandra's head.
and we all know that, once there,
it cannot be dislodged until it has come to fruition.

none the less, we tried our best to dissuade her.
because this idea had only one possible outcome...
chaos.

so, there we were, amy and myself,
innocently going about our routine,
when sandra suddenly said;
"i know what we need to do."

we sort of held our breath,
hoping her mind would jump to a different track.
you can never be certain what is going to follow
"i know what *we* need to do"
except that *we* will soon be doing it.

"let's get big and little and sophie together and take their picture wearing santa hats!"

amy said; "i don't know about that, mom."

i just interjected; "catastrophe."

"well, why not? it will make a nice christmas card."

i looked for the easy way out.
"big would co-operate. we could take big's picture."

"well what about the other dogs? don't they deserve to be in the picture?"

amy tried to help; "i'm not sure it is possible to have all dogs stationary at the same time."

i hopefully tossed in;
"big will work with us."

sandra looked disappointed.

amy made one last attempt;
"it's not that we don't want to do it. it's just that it's the worst idea ever."

"well, i can't understand why y'all won't cooperate for one minute."

i knew what my choices were;
crush sandra's dreams or try to get all three dogs in one picture.

the easy part was getting big.
and little and sophie were already in the pen.
maybe if we took the picture really, really fast...

"big, you want to go sit on the porch?"
big came over and i disconnected his cable.
"go wait on the porch."
big raced to the porch to wait for me.
watching big go past was enough to get sophie and little fully wound, and they began racing around the pen.

i went and sat on the steps and patted beside me.
"come sit here, big."
big came and sat.
so far so good.

amy set up in front of me with her camera,
and sandra went to let sophie and little out.
little was poised at the gate, quivering.
think jack russell. think bull terrier. then multiply them.
it was like watching a nuclear reactor about to melt down.
sophie was spinning in circles.
this was going to be...

interesting.

sandra opened the gate,
and there was that moment of stillness before pandemonium.
then little shot out the gate at 100 miles an hour.
she shot past me and big and disappeared around the corner.
sophie ran straight to big, rolled onto her back, and melted.

amy was trying to pick up a liquid sophie and place her beside
me on the porch.
little shot back past and vanished into the woods.
"call them to you" sandra instructed.
i was putting the santa hat on big.

amy finally got sophie about halfway into a sitting position on
the other side of me from big.
little completed a circle in the woods,
raced up the steps and spun around to race back down and out
into the woods again.
big's santa hat fell off.
"why won't you call them to you?" sandra asked.

sophie took off after little,
then remembered that she knew where big's bone was buried
and raced to dig it out.
littlle shot back past us, and i could hear her breathing hard.
i thought she might have even slowed a little.
maybe in just a minute, we might get a 1 second window.
i put big's santa hat back on.

sophie came running up, proudly carrying big's bone,
and laid down next to amy.
"if you would just call them to you."
amy tried to stop laughing long enough to take the bone from
sophie and push her back on the porch.

"sophie; little; come on girls;"
i called out to two dogs who were beyond hearing anything.
little raced back past us.
she was definitely slowing down now.
i could just catch a glint in the corner of amy's eye,
as the sunlight reflected off a tear.
big's santa hat fell off.

i put big's santa hat back on,
while amy was pushing sophie back up beside me.
while she pushed the front end up, the back end slipped off.
while she heaved the back end up,
the front end slid down.
it was like moving a dog with no bones.
little shot past and started another loop thru the woods.
"just call them to you." came sandra's advice.

amy finally got all of sophie on the step,
and i adjusted big's santa hat before it could fall off again.
then i wrapped an arm around sophie to hold her in place.
little was nearing the completion of another circle,
i could tell that her flywheel was about to wind down.
"little, little, come on little."

little veered off her track and raced up the steps.
i heard the silence as the thunder of her feet finally stopped.
"NOW, NOW!"
i wasn't sure which way little was facing,
but this was probably the best chance we would have.

the pause lasted a mere second or two,
then little shot back down the steps and out into the woods.
sophie squirmed out of my arms and took off after her.
big's santa hat fell off.

"did you get it?" i asked amy.
"i took like 5 pictures" amy responded.
"i think one of them had all 3 dogs in it."

a moment later;
"YES! we have one with all 3 dogs."
"that is probably the best we'll get." i told sandra.
"you should have called them to you."

your christmas card is on big's facebook page.

laz

12-20-12
every day is somebody's day

i guess there is a big front causing winter storms for parts of the
country north of us.
here we just got a mess of rain,
now followed by strong winds.
there is a constant roar of the wind thru the trees.

there was no way to have big's shelter repaired in this weather,
and his area is a muddy mess, anyway.
so i am letting him spend the day up on the porch.
this means staying alert in case someone comes up to the house.

a short while ago i heard big start barking,
and i looked up to see him leave the porch.

it was the meter reader
who i am sure is glad to have that remote reader that he can use
from his truck,
because before i could get out and call big back,
he had run out to meet the truck,
with his hackles raised.
i gotta admit, it is a sight that would intimidate me.
big came right back,
but i reckon that is one more service person definitely not
putting our house on a list to visit later.

while i was out on the back porch,
i heard the two local hawks calling away,
so i looked up to see them both together.
their wings were bowed in sharp crescents,
and they were wheeling, turning, and doing all manner of
aerobatic tricks in the wind.

the winds were so strong,
that they were performing their magic almost in place.
listening to them call,
and watching them perform,
there is no way they weren't just having pure fun.

one of the short creek crows tried to go up and harass them,
but the winds were too much for him,
he had to battle to keep from being blown away,
and he quickly gave it up.
the hawks were in their element.

even the cruddiest day is a great day for somebody.

laz

12-24-12
the big wind

i didn't really appreciate the durability of big's old tarp shelter.
for more than a year and a half it had withstood everything.
rainstorms, windstorms, even two tornados hopping over us.

a weakness had finally shown thru in the fall.
a tiny tear formed and gradually grew until the next major blow
had ripped it in half.
thinking the configuration was the key,
i had gotten big a larger tarp,
and did my best to replicate the layout of the one it replaced.

for a few days he had a primo shelter,
better than the old one.
and then a rain and windstorm tore the corners off.

big is lucky he has so many friends.
his pal tim showed up with a new tarp for him.
i wisely waited for a good day to rebuild,
and a full day of 30 and 40 mile an hour winds demolished what
was left of his old tarp.

the day before yesterday was perfect,
and i spent the afternoon building the finest shelter yet.
it was slanted to enhance rain drainage,
aligned so that the prevalent winds would pass under and out
the other side,
and attached in multiple locations,
so that no single attachment would bear the brunt of any
weather assault.
when i finished i felt confident that this could withstand anything
short of a hurricane.

yesterday morning the shelter got it's first test.
the wind blew.
the rain fell.
the shelter performed just like it was supposed to perform.
it flapped, but the wind didn't catch it full force.
the water flowed off smoothly, without forming puddles.

i gave it one final check before bedtime,
and it appeared to have withstood a day of rain and wind
unscathed.
knowing there would be a break between rainstorms today,
i made plans to go out and reinforce any weaknesses that might
have been exposed.

i woke up at 0400 like normal,
and lay there on my bed listening to the rain.
me and big would be getting a late start this morning.
just before i rolled over to sleep a little longer,
a barely audible sound caught my attention.
it sounded like a distant freight train.

as i listened to the rapid crescendo of noise,
i thought of the two possible sources
(since i was fairly certain no one had lain railroad tracks next to
the house during the night)
there was either a huge deluge of rain approaching thru the
woods, or some sort of freak windburst.
given that it was not windy, i waited for a downpour.

the sound grew until it was almost deafening,
and then suddenly a wind hit the house with an impact i could
feel.
i could hear the windows bang against the inside of their frames,
and the rain hitting the panes sounded like gravels.
the roar had grown to the intensity of a jet engine.
the house shuddered under the force.
i could hear and feel the wind start to let up,
and then it would hit again with renewed force.
i seriously wondered if the windows would be blown in.

it seemed like it went on for 10 minutes,
altho reflecting on it later,
i wondered if it actually lasted as long as 30 seconds.
as suddenly as it had hit, it was gone.
the house actually settled back from the pressure,
and i could hear the receding roar of the wind.
i started to settle in for my bonus snooze,
and then i remembered big's new tarp.

it was a couple of hours before it got light enough to see.
as soon as there was any light at all,
i could see big's tarp was not all right.
once there was good light,
i could see that it had been absolutely shredded.
the inside of his house was soaked.

the wierdest part,
was that it was not windy before that thing hit,
and it was not windy after.
it was like a blast of wind that came especially for big's tarp.

when we went out walking after the rain stopped,
there was not even any wind damage around the neighborhood.

i am not going anywhere near a store on christmas eve.
i reckon big has a couple of days on the porch in his immediate
future.
i have to find someplace that sells the real tarps;
made of canvas...

i only hope if i find one,
it won't attract an even stronger windburst.

laz

12-27-12
the coyote hunters

i'm pretty sure we saw them before they saw us.

me and big were nearing the end of our walk,
with the morning twilight just beginning to illuminate big
territory.
we had been talking about the seasons.

i was bundled up against the morning chill
(big, of course, was loving the cold wind in his face)
winter solstice had officially arrived a week ago,
but it never really feels like winter in these parts until january.

we had talked about how fall and spring seem to arrive on a
specific day,
when me and big can feel it in our bones that the season has
changed.
but summer and winter sort of slide into place.
one day we just realize that the seasons have changed,
almost unnoticed.

we speculated on why the solar cycle does not match up exactly
with the seasons.
logically, it wold seem like the longest day of the year would be
the warmest, and the shortest day of the year would be the
coldest, with the temperatures graduating between the two
extremes according to the length of the days.
instead, the longest and shortest days fall at the beginning of
warm and cold weather.

i tried to explain to big about the effects of ocean currents,
and the jet stream,
but i could tell i had lost him.
big was much more interested in:
where a racoon had crossed the road during the night,
a new fast-food sack in the ditch,
and the pickup truck slowly approaching.

the old truck was coming towards us in our lane,
so me and big switched sides of the road.

we not only know all the cars that we normally see in big
territory, but the times that we see them.
this strange vehicle, at an odd hour, moving slowly,
piqued our interest.

since they had their lights on,
the men in the truck probably didn't see us until they had almost
reached us.
the truck slowed to a stop,
and the driver greeted me;
"hi; i'm bob and this is john...we're coyote hunters."
"hey; i'm laz...and i'm walking."
(you look like coyote hunters, i thought)

about that time, big stood up on his hind legs to see who it was.
at the sight of big's massive head suddenly looking him in the
eye, the coyote hunter drew back, startled.

"is that a good dog?"
"yeah, he's as good as they come."
i immediately regretted saying it.
i didn't know these two guys,
and i worry about my good-natured fella falling in the wrong
hands.
the coyote hunter patted big's massive head,
and big wagged his tail.
then he dropped to the ground to wait on us getting back to
work.

"we're here to clean out the coyotes."
i had my doubts about that.
growing up out west, i was very familiar with coyotes.
they are smart and resourceful.
despite facing guns, poison, and traps,
the coyotes flourished.
some places they were even hunted from airplanes.

coyotes had not even arrived in tennessee until the 1980's.
since that time,
the most determined efforts had not "cleaned them out."
it had not even stopped them from spreading to every corner of
the state.

me and big sometimes listen to the coyotes at night.
big smells where they have been while we are walking,
and sometimes we see their tracks in the snow or the mud.
once in a while we even spot one.
but we do not know where they stay.
coyotes are elusive.
i doubted that the coyote hunters would have much effect on the
coyote population.
i could only hope they would not be shooting indiscriminately,
or scattering poison.

"where do you live?"
"down the road a ways."
that was as revealing as i cared to get with these two.
if the evasive answer bothered them, it didn't show.
"mr winston is letting us hunt on his property."
i just nodded.
"we can take care of the coyotes for you."
"they don't bother me."

"just don't forget that me and big are out before sunup a lot."

the coyote hunters went on their way.
me and big went on ours.

it is going to be an interesting winter in big territory.

laz

Enjoy this book?

This is the fourth book of The Big Dog Diaries. Come back for book 5, which will cover Winter and Spring of The Big Year.

About the Author

Lazarus Lake did not write this book; he merely recorded the stories that Big shared with him. They live on a small farm in Tennessee where they train and organize popular ultra-marathons, a world-wide community that Laz has been a part of for over 3 decades and Big first joined a couple of years ago.

Made in the USA
Charleston, SC
07 October 2014